GENERAL EDITOR: DEREK BLOWS
New Library of Pastoral Care

Derek Blows is the Director of the Westminster Pastoral
Foundation and a psychotherapist at University College
Hospital. He is also an honorary canon of Southwark
Cathedral.

The Pastor as Theologian

Titles in this series include:

GENERAL EDITOR: DEREK BLOWS
New Library of Pastoral Care

———

THE PASTOR AS THEOLOGIAN

*The Integration of Pastoral Ministry,
Theology and Discipleship*

———

Wesley Carr

First published in Great Britain 1989
SPCK
Holy Trinity Church
Marylebone Road
London NW1 4DU

British Library Cataloguing in Publication Data

Carr, Wesley, *1941—*
    The pastor as theologian: the integration
    of pastoral ministry, theology and
    discipleship.
    1. Christian church. Pastoral work
    I. Title   II. Series
    253
    ISBN 0-281-04391-4

Filmset by Pioneer
**Printed and bound in Great Britain by
Anchor Press Ltd, Tiptree, Essex**

*For
Natalie*

Contents

PART TWO
Exploring the Issues

Contents

CONCLUSION

Foreword

The *New Library of Pastoral Care* has been planned to meet the needs of those people concerned with pastoral care, whether clergy or lay, who seek to improve their knowledge and skills in this field. Equally, it is hoped that it may prove useful to those secular helpers who may wish to understand the role of the pastor.

Pastoral care in every age has drawn from contemporary secular knowledge to inform its understanding of man and his various needs and of the ways in which these needs might be met. Today it is perhaps the secular helping professions of social work, counselling and psychotherapy, and community development which have particular contributions to make to the pastor in his work. Such knowledge does not stand still, and a pastor would have a struggle to keep up with the endless tide of new developments which pour out from these and other disciplines, and to sort out which ideas and practices might be relevant to his particular pastoral needs. Among present-day ideas, for instance, of particular value might be an understanding of the social context of the pastoral task, the dynamics of the helping relationship, the attitudes and skills as well as factual knowledge which might make for effective pastoral intervention and, perhaps most significant of all, the study of particular cases, whether through verbatim reports of interviews or general case presentation. The discovery of ways of learning from what one is doing is becoming increasingly important.

There is always a danger that a pastor who drinks deeply at the well of a secular discipline may lose his grasp of his own pastoral identity and become 'just another' social worker or counsellor. It in no way detracts from the value of these professions to assert that the role and task of the pastor are quite unique among the helping professions and deserve to be clarified and strengthened rather than weakened. The theological commitment of the pastor and the appropriate use of his role will be a recurrent theme of the series. At the same time the pastor cannot afford to work in a vacuum. He needs to be able to communicate and co-operate with those helpers in other disciplines whose work may overlap, without loss of his own unique role. This in turn will mean being able to communicate with them through some understanding of their concepts and language.

Finally, there is a rich variety of styles and approaches in pastoral work within the various religious traditions. No attempt will be made to secure a uniform approach. The Library will contain the variety, and even perhaps occasional eccentricity, which such a title suggests. Some books will be more specifically theological and others more concerned with particular areas of need or practice. It is hoped that all of them will have a usefulness that will reach right across the boundaries of religious denomination.

DEREK BLOWS
Series Editor

Preface

On the seashore of endless worlds, children play . . .
(Rabindranath Tagore [Winnicott 1971, 95])

The Sea of Faith
Was once, too, at the full, and round earth's shore
Lay like the folds of a bright girdle furl'd.
But now I only hear
Its melancholy, long, withdrawing roar,
Retreating, to the breath
Of the night-wind, down the vast edges drear
And naked shingles of the world.
(Matthew Arnold, Dover Beach)

What psychoanalysis can never do is determine whether, after all
the psychodynamic factors are removed, there is an ultimate
justification for religious faith.
[Wallace 1983, 280]

Never before had so many seen man's shortcomings so clearly, and
been able to do so little about it.
[Becker 1964, 200]

Attempting to write an integrating work is like standing on the beach as the surging waves of what seem like original ideas break on the pages' shore. Some disappoint, their apparent magnificence quietly dissolving. Others overwhelm, crashing through ordered argument and previously secure assumptions. One moment the sea is inviting and seductive; splashing around the fringes of the profound issues of life and death, we write our intentions in the sand, hoping that they will be washed away and not held to our account. The next moment we are caught in the current and washed out to sea. The horizon retreats beyond our reach and our feet cannot touch the bottom.

The quotations at the top of the previous page remind the reader that the first move in examining Christian theology, discipleship and pastoral ministry together has to be to stand on the beach. Two academic theologians have recently urged this stance with their use of Matthew Arnold's wistfulness in *Dover Beach*: Don Cupitt, in his television series and accompanying book *Sea of Faith,* and Nicholas Lash, in his collection of essays entitled *Theology on Dover Beach.* (Christian discipleship undoubtedly begins at the seaside: 'As Jesus was walking beside the sea . . . he saw Simon and his brother Andrew . . . He said to them, "Follow me"' (Mark 1.16 – 17).) But does the sea appear inviting or threatening to pastors? So far as I know, the image has not been specifically applied to the Churches' pastoral work. But many sensitive pastors today feel at sea. The familiar horizons seem to become more distant as assumptions about the Church and the contexts in which it works are challenged and adjusted. At the same time the sands begin to shift under our feet.

Turmoil in theology is not confined to universities and colleges. If it were, most Churches and Christians would probably, as always, be largely unperturbed. The dilemma is more acute: in many ways we know more about our world and ourselves than our predecessors knew. But knowledge does not necessarily lead to competent living. All are caught between relevance and identity; the pastor is bound to feel this, for his ministry must be relevant to people and their predicaments, and it is based upon whatever sense of identity as Christian minister he can develop and which others can discern.

The aim of this book is to open up for pastors some of the problems, but also opportunities, that are theirs when they hold together three perspectives: the Christian theological stances which they have inherited and in various ways made their own; their ministry to people who share neither the theology nor the way of discipleship; and the practice of Christian discipleship. The technical problems of interdisciplinary writing, therefore, are not faced by the author alone. They represent what pastors experience in their day-to-day work: How am I to offer counsel or interpretation, ritual or ceremony, in terms which are faithful to the gospel for which I stand and sufficiently congruent with the world-views and value-systems of those with whom I am ministering? The alert pastor cannot escape from this struggle. Nor can anyone who tries to reflect upon that ministry.

Inevitably, therefore. this book is difficult in places. I can only ask readers to hold on through the gales in the hope that a lifebelt of something familiar will be thrown before they sink. This might be an insight about ourselves, a familiar theological idea, a text of Scripture, or a story of pastoral practice. My only guarantee is that all these do occur in the text.

One or two practical points remain to be explained. On the whole I have used the words 'pastor' and 'minister' interchangeably, and from time to time employed other terms. It will become obvious that, while I frequently have in mind the publicly recognizable ministers of churches, I am not here concerned about questions of ordination and other issues, such as the ministry of the laity and/or that of the clergy. Ministry is defined in terms of what other people request or demand, and what, therefore, they may or may not allow a minister, ordained or not, to perform. This functional aspect to questions of orders and authorization is underestimated in many of today's arguments about the Churches' ministries. But it is a daily reality to living churches and working ministers.

Questions of gender are unimportant in the context of this book, although I have tried to acknowledge them. A major problem, however, occurs when we speak of the individual. Some sentences cannot be rendered in the plural without changing the meaning, and the repetition of 'he and she' or neologisms like '(s)he' are both in their different ways burdensome. I have done my best within the constraints of language.

No book is as original as the author thinks. The ideas of many, and probably their words too, are inadvertently used. But some people make particular contributions, with ideas, stories and encouragement to keep struggling. So I specially thank several good friends and colleagues: Michael Fox, Rector of St James's, Colchester, Tim Stevens, the Bishop of Chelmsford's Adviser on Urban Priority Areas, and Peter

Marshall, Canon Residentiary of Ripon Cathedral, as well as numerous people with whom I have worked on studies with the Tavistock Institute of Human Relations and its counterpart in the USA—the centres of the A. K. Rice Institute. My collaborator in various studies, Edward R. Shapiro, Director of the Adolescent and Family Treatment and Study Center, McLean Hospital, Boston, and a practising psychoanalyst—surprised, I suspect, to find himself working with an Anglican priest—has enlivened many hours of debate, argument and joint working, the effects of which also show here. I also thank Judith Longman, Editorial Director of SPCK, for her willingness to spare time for a bewildered author and sustain encouragement. To these named contributors should be linked a host of others with whom I have worked over recent years. None of them, however, should be held responsible for what appears here.

WESLEY CARR
January 1988
Bristol Cathedral

A Note on References

I have kept notes and references to a minimum, but in presenting them I have adopted a convention which has not yet been widely used in writing on theology and pastoralia. References are incorporated in the text and can be pursued through the Bibliography, which includes only books and articles that are mentioned in the text. So, for example, a reference appears in the text thus:

'. . . sometimes consciously, sometimes unconsciously' [Rycroft 1985, 26].

Rycroft refers to the author listed;

1985 identifies the date of publication and, therefore, the particular book or article against Rycroft's name;

26 tells which page is being directly quoted. Where the reference is more general, this number is missing.

PART ONE

Discovering a Contemporary Perspective

ONE

Introduction

_____

One day Socrates made a young slave the centrepiece of a dialogue. Contrasting the innocent and ignorant boy with the sophisticated citizens, Socrates argued that 'a man who does not know, has in himself true opinions on a subject without having knowledge' (Plato _Meno_ 85c). Theologians are in a similar position, and none more so than the practising minister. He has constantly to admit to people that he does not know; but at the same time he claims to have true opinions on human life, the nature of God, and the significance of both.

It is a curious thing that in England — not least in the Church of England, which prides itself on its pastoral activity — the notion of the pastor as theologian does not receive much attention. Pastoral studies, in spite of recent efforts to integrate them into training syllabuses in colleges, courses and seminaries, are still widely assumed to be what the ordinand studies _after_ he has learnt some theology. Even when attempts are made to locate these studies at the heart of the training programme, difficulty is experienced in linking the psychological and sociological perspectives on individuals, groups and organizations with the study of theology [Baelz 1985]. There is little available writing which gives theological value to the actual beliefs and unbeliefs of ordinary people or to the experience of the minister as he struggles to offer Christian interpretations to people's everyday experiences. Yet pastors are theologians of living churches. They need ways of integrating their pastoral experience and practice with the Christian belief that makes them ministers in the first place. A priority, therefore, not least during the changes that churches and communities are today undergoing, is to discover means of holding together these various facets of ministry in an integrating framework. This should not be

3

confused, however, with an integrated framework. Any such thing might seem to be avoiding contemporary confusion and so will to the practising pastor feel (and in fact, be) suspect.

The Context of Ministry

Today we struggle to discover the shape that theological questions and insights may have to adopt in these final years of the twentieth century. The visions presented by recent scientific discovery, for example, seem too vast to be easily incorporated into the structures which have served the Church. Hitherto man and his existence have been the starting- and finishing-points: we begin with Adam and end with the consummation of all things in the new Adam. But the measure is now changing. We are offered maps of the period from the moment of creation until mankind's evolution and subsequent history. And from time to time we glimpse an end in ultimate catastrophe, a matter which has until now fed our imagination but remained beyond our comprehension. This generation does not have to imagine; we have seen. The time-scale and perspective of our lives are altered.

Our sense of order has also changed. Probability and chance are more prominent. Macrocosmic speculation and microcosmic investigation together yield phenomena and ideas which were until recently inconceivable. All this poses questions to the theologian—not an over-simplified dispute between science and religion, but profound questions about what may be thought, how it may be expressed, and whether there is any possibility of integration in our complex, fragmented world.

There is a parallel ferment in the study of ourselves. Research into human behaviour is a dominant factor in twentieth-century thought. Indeed it might be fairly claimed that it is *the* dominant factor. Psychology and sociology influence other disciplines and powerfully affect popular beliefs. The way in which people regard and understand relationships has changed and is changing. The process of believing itself becomes a prominent issue. It is explored in complex contexts as psychologists, psychiatrists, anthropologists and sociologists map the human terrain of individuals, groups, communities and societies. This work has a far-reaching and controversial impact on all professions and systems of thought. The Church and theology are not excluded.

More specifically, there is a range of psychoanalytically derived stances which informs our ways of approaching issues. Some regard the whole psychoanalytic scheme as a deception or distortion [Farrell 1981; Bateson 1972]. The argument rages, and no doubt will continue to do so. The pastor and theologian, however, might note Niebuhr's comment that psychoanalysis might also recapture some of the ideas of the Judaeo-Christian tradition of which the Churches have lost sight [Niebuhr 1964]. Although the practice of analysis may need to be modified, it seems that psychoanalytically informed approaches have a sound base and that they will continue to contribute to styles of thought and life which already profoundly affect people.

The concept of pastoral ministry itself has undergone a similar upheaval. Some ministers have sought refuge in sectarian behaviour, locking themselves into the life of a congregation and its idiosyncratic activities. Others, confronted with demands too big to comprehend, have felt unsure about any distinctively Christian ministry and so have used their independence to create a counselling service or to engage in some kind of social work [Carr 1985a]. Neither activity is wrong in itself; but each in its own way implicitly finds unsatisfactory some facet of the Christian gospel, which does not claim to be solely concerned with either God or with our neighbour.

The problem facing any minister working in this ferment is therefore that of integration: how is he to hold together the three facets of his daily activity for which he is publicly accountable to others, because he is available for their scrutiny; for which he is privately examinable, like anyone else, by himself; and for which he stands distinctively under the judgement of God? These three parts are:

1. The practice of pastoral ministry through care for others and interpretation. This is always a demand on a minister's sensitivity. It is more so today, however, because of the eruption in our Western societies of caring agencies, which

are freely available and which create and respond to a culture dominated by psychological assumptions.

2. The theological undergirding of his grasp of the mystery of God in a systematic exploration of the Christian faith:

> It is said that souls are not saved nor the Kingdom advanced by academic rigour, intellectual openness or the need to ask the awkward question. True enough. But without the infrastructure of rigorous theological exploration and intellectual openness, evangelism and mission are all too likely to run out into the sands of irrelevance or superstition, bigotry or fanaticism. [Baker 1986, 349]

The pastor as local theologian has to embody this stance in himself as he holds the mystery of God present to the everyday lives of ordinary men and women, believer and unbeliever alike.

3. Maintenance of distinctively Christian life in both himself and those with whom he shares his ministry. Today's Churches are distinguished by a concern with liturgy, although this seems to drift towards the myth that if we can recover something from the past it necessarily contributes to the present. This public, corporate expression of Christian life in worship is matched by anxieties about private devotion. The minister is required both to be an example of one who prays and to teach prayer to others. The practice of the Christian life is spirituality, a vogue word of the present. And evangelism is also urged upon him and he is made to feel responsible for this.

Each of these topics is the pastor's daily concern and each brings its own anxieties. But it is all the more important that they should be brought together, if they are to inform each other and if ministers are to remain integrated people. How pastors operate in their complex role is crucial for the development of the Christian Church, its theology, liturgy and pastoral practice. Yet although studies abound on each of the topics, few offer an integrating model by which the pastor might live competently in the modern world which is informed by psychology, the troubled world of systematic theology and the changing world of Christian practice, without fleeing from one or all of these.

Interdisciplinary Study

The amalgam of life, belief and pastoral practice requires interdisciplinary effort on the part of any writer. I have tried to make use of systematic theology and psychoanalytic ideas as the two primary disciplines. Both, of course, are suspect with different groups of people. The pitfalls here are so deep that anyone is bound to fall into them and be duly criticized. As a pre-emptive defence, therefore, I offer three statements.

First, the theologies discussed in this book are not intended to be complete. Although they concern three primary Christian doctrines, like all working theologies they are partial, limited and to a degree *ad hoc*. Zechariah's exhortation not to 'despise the day of small things' (Zech. 4.10) might today be revised to 'Do not be afraid of fragmentary theologies.' One criterion of any theology which a working minister can and will explore, is whether it is useful in enabling him to discover order in the welter of his pastoral experience. A second would be whether it is communicable, either through the style of that pastoral activity or in direct proclamation of the Christian gospel. For that reason I have included stories and each chapter on pastoral activity contains a case study.

Second, my aim is to clarify contemporary theological thinking, pastoral requirements and the Church and its distinctive practices, and to show that there are links between them. These derive chiefly from the obvious fact that all in their various ways are concerned with the same source of primary data—people. This is where some psychodynamic material and ideas are needed, not because psychoanalysis and its derivatives are beyond question, but because psycho-analytically informed ways of thinking are now, even if all do not consciously realize it, a principal contributor to the way people today conceive of themselves and perceive their world.

When in the second part of the book we turn to three major theological themes, lines of connection can be discerned between the issues with which Christian theologians have struggled, the pastoral demands that are made on the Church and its ministers, and particular aspects of the Church's internal life. For example, the doctrine of the atonement illuminates our handling of the human propensity to ambiguity and ambivalence, and theological questioning and pastoral practice together lead to reflections on the nature of today's Christian spirituality.

Third, what is attempted here has to be tried. There seems little doubt that the Christian Church, at least in this country, is finding difficulty in staying in touch with those among whom it ministers and witnesses. Gaps emerge between professed doctrine (which often looks like a demand for credulity before the grace of God can be experienced) and religious sensitivities on the part of many people. The Christian interpretation of human life is not commending itself. Yet our symbols and myths — crucifixion, resurrection, baptism, and so on — remain powerful and are widely employed. This again is the world of the public minister and pastor, whose professionalism has to be discovered, exercised and refined in this environment. A cohering way of thinking is essential. This book merely offers a first effort at something that is important.

Psychoanalysis and Christian Practice

Freud and his successors have shifted our perspectives so that the framework with which we think about life has been profoundly altered. Mention of Freud's name (interestingly, this is less true of Jung's) arouses anxiety in some pastors. It is, therefore, worth recalling at the outset that, although Freud sometimes may appear anti-religious, one of his earliest and lifelong friends was a practising Christian pastor — Oskar Pfister. He acknowledged the significance of Freud's seminal thinking, taking it into his pastoral practice and feeding the results back to Freud [Meng & Freud 1963]. Yet he opted to remain in his world of applied theology. Although they differed in their assessment of religion, Freud and Pfister remained intimate friends for thirty years, a high point in their relationship occurring when, in response to Freud's *The Future of an Illusion* [1927], Pfister produced *The Illusion of the Future* [1928]. Here, as in their correspondence, the two discussed the application of psychoanalysis to the Church's pastoral practice and the theoretical basis of this new discipline. Although Pfister, so far as we know, seems not to have made direct links between psychoanalytical insights and any consequential development that might be required in Christian theological thought, such questions seem to have arisen in their discussions.

In spite of this early association between pastoral practice, theology and psychoanalysis, less attention has been paid to the impact on theology of this dimension of modern thought than has been the case with the natural and physical sciences. One reason for this may be the covert assumption that those who care need not grapple with ways of integrating their theological understanding with their pastoral activity. In the face of a world increasingly dominated by bureaucracies and technologies, the image of a Christ who neither created an organization nor developed a theological system has become attractive. The Church's structures and intellectual formulations may become obsolete but 'the life of actual loving and caring, guided by tested knowledge, cannot get out of date' [Guntrip 1971, 14]. Such an observation invites assent. But the illegitimate conclusion may sometimes be drawn that there does not have to be a link between the practice of pastoral ministry and the theological understanding that undergirds it. Unless, however, the theology that informs the practice of ministry is recognizably congruent with the theoretical world which illuminates its pastoral practice, the Church will prove hypocritical—that is, as holding at its heart two incompatible ways of thinking.

It might, however, be suggested that this disaster can occur only if the Church surrenders its pastoral practice to analytically informed approaches. These, therefore, should be abandoned so that in one move we rescue both theology and the pastoral stance. But however much we question psychoanalytical approaches, it is impossible to escape their influence. Some components have rightly attained secure status. To retreat from these, however many of the ideas that have accrued around them we modify or discard, is to opt out of the only world that we have—the contemporary one. What is more, since these ideas themselves, often in an attenuated or debased form, permeate contemporary thinking and behaviour to an extraordinary degree, the minister needs to be aware of and, to some extent, to engage with them as a prerequisite of pastoral work. People are not blanks on to which ideas are painted. They share in and contribute to that *mélange* of ideas which produces the ambience in which life is lived and interpreted. So long as they wish to work with people, pastors cannot reject these approaches, however critical they may become of them.

A further limitation may arise from the unfortunate antipathy that has been set up between some writers on analysis and some theologians. For example, Reuben Fines baldly states that psychoanalysis is the dominant intellectual force of the twentieth century. It rejects religion as a desirable influence in human existence. Darwin's attack (*sic*) on religious thinking led to the dissolution of Scripture in the acids of criticism; Freudian analysis has exposed unjustifiable practices in religion and shown that religious experience is a neurosis. The social justification of religion as a unifying force is an illusion. Religion is merely a form of psychotherapy which functions as magic. As a result, it should play no role in 'the psychoanalytic vision of happiness' [Fines 1981, 261].

In the face of this type of attack, which so defines the field as to be unanswerable, it is not surprising that professional theologians tend to reply with an attentive exegesis of Freud's texts. They try to determine the precise meaning of what he wrote, expose internal inconsistencies, and look for loopholes which they can exploit. Hans Küng, for example, offers a masterly study, which sets Freud's ideas about God in their nineteenth-century context [Küng 1983]. But the result is a sterile debate based on past issues. Two impressive minds meet but do not engage.

This happens because of the crucial decision to discount therapeutic questions. Although some try to separate theory from the practice of interpretation with patients, psychoanalysis is a practice rather than a theory. Its theoretical exploration has to be based on case studies, just as any therapeutic or pastoral stance has to be concerned with the person who is here and now present. Time in this context is not linear, but circular, revolving around the patient. Although the process moves back and forth through time, history—in the sense of an assured, discoverable past—is not a factor. 'Interpretation is a particularised creative action, performed within a tradition of procedure and understanding. It has no beginning and no end' [Schafer 1978, 13]. The general influence of psychoanalytic theory on thought, including theology, cannot be determined, understood or discussed from texts or the history of the development of ideas alone.

The analytic process itself inhibits such a response and makes it irrelevant. Indeed the easiest work of Freud to refute is that where he speculates about the origins of religion. But when analytic thinking deals with religion's experiential aspects and its continuing potency, Christians and theologians, as participants in the contemporary world, have to engage with it. What is more, this sense of immediacy corresponds precisely to the oft-repeated demand of the pastor as theologian that he has to live in the here and now, with a faith that can be grasped and used by those whom he meets. It cannot, therefore, in the end be a matter only of history or philosophy. His critical factor, like that of the analyst, is continuity—a process of moving back and forth through history, between moments of divine revelation and similar moments today.

The question, therefore, that we have to address is how to relate our contemporary pastoral practice (informed as it is by various psychological insights and stances) to our primary point of reference—our theological understanding. We have no option but to study how they interrelate and illuminate each other.

The Pastor's Theology

I am attempting to outline some aspects of systematic theology from a pastoral perspective that is informed by psychoanalytic ideas. This style of working is similar to that espoused by the writers of doxological theology. They take Christian worship— a central, definable area of Christian life—as the key factor. It is the point at which the vision of the Christian community is most sharply focused. The theologian, with his assigned task of eliciting and elucidating doctrine, can use this to further his work. The result is a rewarding study, which both opens up new perspectives on Christian doctrine and enlivens the Church's liturgical life [Wainwright 1980].

In our study we shall take another primary area of Christian life—pastoral practice. Whereas, however, worship is central to the Church's life, pastoral ministry is exercised at its margins, where belief coincides with unbelief and half-belief, and where the gospel's adequacy is constantly tested. Uncertainties, rather than assurances, are the norm. So any theological enterprise based on them is likely to be hazardous and frequently dubious. Nevertheless, this attempt draws into the core of theological reflection a formative area of the Church's life. For if there is no ministry with people other than believers, the Church's claim to a message of universal significance fails.

Before embarking further on this enterprise, we need to establish the type of theology being attempted. Like pastors, theologians cannot escape the complex social reality in which they and their audiences are set [Gill 1975; Gill 1977]. If they do, there results 'a relaxed, if not lazy, pluralism contenting itself with sharing private stories, while both the authentically public character of every good story and the real needs of the wider society go unremarked' [Tracy 1981, 204].

It is not easy to attempt this public enterprise by taking account of the current environment and trying to contribute something to it. We can see the problem when we examine the range of adjectives which are used with 'theology': natural, systematic, fundamental, dogmatic, applied, philosophical, biblical, and many more. In the face of such an onslaught, we might follow Tracy's suggestion of an alternative set of categories: orthodox, neo-orthodox, liberal, radical and revisionist. To these we can add the modern fashion of speaking of a theology *of* something: the theology of work, the theology of the laity, and so on. But then the word becomes so elastic that it might be used with almost anything. On top of this, it is impossible to ignore the inelegant, but suggestive and widely used phrase, 'doing theology'. With so great an array of options, some definition of 'theology' is needed to get our study under way. What sort of theology are we attempting, and to which public are we primarily addressing it?

The list — orthodox, neo-orthodox, etc. — describes a series of models for theological thinking which have been determined by different intellectual and social cultures. As existing frameworks of thought become ineffective in the society of which the Church is part, and inadequate to sustain the inner experience of the Church's members, new responses develop. Barth's *The Epistle to the Romans*, especially the second edition of 1922, is a good example: 'All unaware, I had been allowed to take a step which many people had been waiting for and to do things for which many people were prepared' [Busch 1976, 120]. Or we might compare John Robinson's response to the debate on *Honest to God*: 'The hundreds of letters I have received, particularly from the younger generation, inside the Church and out of it, have convinced me that I may have rung a bell for others too' [Robinson 1963, 279]. Such theologies depend upon their outworking in a particular culture and public, and on their interaction with them. But they cannot be intentionally constructed. As Barth and Robinson show, they emerge from a struggle and are confirmed in retrospect.

The other set of terms—natural, systematic, etc.—offers more immediate scope. From this list Tracy extracts three main types of theologies and the publics to which they are directed: fundamental, systematic and practical. Fundamental theology (which includes natural, apologetic and philosophical theology) addresses the academy; systematic theology operates with the community of moral and religious discourse, the Church; practical theology is concerned with society at large. Each has its own style of working. Fundamental theology deals in rationality and argument. By contrast, systematic theologians are concerned with 'the reinterpretation of what is assumed to be the ever present and disclosive and transformative power of the particular religious tradition to which the theologian belongs' [Tracy 1981, 54]. Practical theology is caught up in social, political and pastoral concerns.

In this study we are occupied with the second category, systematic theology. The public addressed is firstly the Church, since the underlying concern is the potentially disastrous split that may emerge for ministers between pastoral practice and theological understanding. The nature of the material, however, ensures that there must be practical outcomes. That is as it should be. For while these categories are useful for clarifying a focus, there is inevitably an overlap between them, especially between systematic and practical theology. This connection is strengthened when the primary data derives from the pastoral experiences of the living Church. Such an approach may, and in practice often does, degenerate into an anecdotally supported exposition of prejudices. To escape that fate we have also to discover a model which can be used to interpret the connections between pastoral data and our theological enterprise.

Conclusion

My aim, therefore, is to help working pastors to integrate their pastoral experience and practice with their professed systematic theology and their religious activity in worship, prayer and spirituality. Pastoral activity and human experience together are inevitably the most pressing concerns for any pastor. Formal academic study is squeezed out by the competing demands for pastoral ministry and congregational service. It therefore seems wise to take an approach to understanding human behaviour and relations as a suitable ground on which to seek this integration. That is today largely informed by psychoanalytic insights. The form of the argument is simple.

First we establish a way of thinking and talking about God and religious experience in an analytically informed context without abandoning faith in God. There is a brief discussion on analytical developments and their significance, followed by clarification of some basic concepts. The bulk of the book consists of theological, pastoral and religious reflections on three core doctrines of the Christian faith—incarnation, atonement and creation/resurrection. The term to describe these—'classic'—is taken from Tracy. Several doctrines might claim such status, and the choice of three may seem arbitrary, but as Tracy himself writes: 'On inner-Christian grounds there is one classic event and person which normatively judges and informs all other Christian classics, and which serves as the classic Christian focus for understanding God, self, others, society, history, nature and the whole Christianly: the event and person of Jesus Christ' [Tracy 1981, 233].

In each chapter we shall examine how a Christian classic may be reinterpreted in the light of the human dynamics that we have uncovered. In so doing, I hope to show that there is grounding in theology for attitudes derived from pastoral practice, and that these can be subjected to a relevant and coherent theological critique. Each classic, it will emerge, is also intimately connected with a fundamental facet of religious behaviour, which is naturally explored in terms of Christian discipleship. An inner connection can thus be demonstrated between the pastoral approach to human beings, the theological interpretation of Christian classics and the foundations of religious behaviour—worship, prayer and spirituality (A schematic outline of the plan will be found in the Conclusion, p. 221).

TWO

Children's Play: The Value of Illusion

I do not know what I may appear to the world, but to myself I seem to have been only a boy playing on the sea-shore. (Isaac Newton [Brewster 1855, *ii.ch.27*])

The context of today's pastoral ministry is permeated by ideas which originate in psychology and psychoanalysis. Ministers and those with whom they work are equally affected. Freud's thought, and that of his successors, runs through the assumptive world of everyday life. Young mothers, for example, base the way they care for their children on psychological insights, albeit corrupted and, from the purist's perspective, debased. For many of them books have supplanted wisdom inherited from their mother. Even the speed with which one theory replaces another does not seem to diminish the belief that properly to bring up a baby you need an approach informed by modern psychology. If, therefore, we are to develop a theological stance which is congruent with the demands of pastoral ministry and which takes seriously the context in which it is exercised, we must look at some of Freud's thinking, especially with regard to religion.

To move confidently into this field we need to set aside the anxiety that mention of Freud and psychoanalysis sometimes generates in pastors. Psychological triumphalism, by which it appears to offer an explanation for every aspect of human life, including a dismissive one for religion, can have a debilitating effect on ministers. They begin to recall their predecessors' power, which in fantasized retrospect seems to have been surrendered to therapists and analysts. We need, therefore, to be clear about the material that we are handling and to be reassured both of its strengths and possibilities, as well as being realistic about its limitations.

Religious and Common Human Experience

Freud and some of his successors have described religion as an *illusion*, although in practice they treat it as a *delusion*. The difference is important. Illusions are a key ingredient in ordinary human existence and functioning. They always need examining, but their psychological legitimacy is not in doubt. Delusions, by contrast, call for treatment. We human beings live in our real world through illusion, by which we structure and give meaning and sustenance to our existence. By contrast, delusion involves losing touch with reality. One reason why the two are confused is that psychoanalytically informed authors tend to restrict religious phenomena to 'religious experience'. This is then described in terms of visions, conversion-experiences or mysticism, which are taken to indicate hallucinations or some kind of psychosis and are summed up as delusional.

Freud, for example, expounds this view of religion in *Civilisation and Its Discontents*, although in true nineteenth-century style conceding it some social utility:

> [Religion] depresses the value of life and distorts the picture of the real world in a delusional manner, which presupposes an intimidation of the intelligence. At this price, by forcibly fixing them in a state of psychical infantilism and by drawing them into a mass delusion, religion succeeds in sparing many people an individual neurosis. [Freud 1930, 34]

There is no obvious way to respond to this argument, so long as we isolate the phenomenon of religious experience. In terms of this theory, all claims to religious experience in these prescribed forms—visions, conversion or mysticism—may be analysed as delusions or, more precisely, as paranoid delusional states. But there is no need to accept the strait-jacket in the first place.

Believers are usually unwilling, and even unable, to distinguish their religious experiences from an all-pervading sense of God or of a notion of otherness. There is personal affirmation and motivation—'I believe' or 'Here I stand'—and the sense of having no choice. The unwilling soul surrendering to the persistent love of God is a standard theme in spiritual experience. The sense of vocation, or of being chosen, even against one's will, predominates. In, for example, the Christian tradition people like St Paul express continuing surprise at finding themselves Christians (Acts 22; Acts 26; Gal. 1.13 — 24). Even Jesus is presented as being chosen in spite of himself and apparently against his will (Mark 14.32 — 36). This enigmatic claim is central to the idea of religious experience.

Similar examples can also be found in other faiths [Bowker 1978]. There is no single experience which can confidently be termed 'religious'. People who believe in God and who for whatever reason become psychotic are likely to express their delusions in religious language. But it does not follow from this that religious experience or the sense of God is to be accounted a delusion. To focus upon religious experience is either to restrict the field of study to states which are inevitably amenable to interpretation as delusional or so to define religion that believers, being unable to discover any of their experience in the definition, are unable to take part in the dialogue.

But if we are not to be confined to specific, claimed religious experiences, then we have to locate belief, its practice and effects, within the sphere of common human experience. The danger here is that we may generalize and implicitly convert all human beings into religious people. If all life is 'religious', what then is the particular phenomenon of 'religion'? Other problems arise from such a generalization about the status of belief and, more importantly, about the nature of religious truth. To avoid this trap we must construe religious experiences to which people lay claim within the context of human experience in general, and study this.

There is no obvious connection between public expression of belief — for example, church attendance — and the remarkable number of people who admit to some sort of religious dimension to their everyday experience [Hay 1982]. The phenomenon of religion remains significant as a factor of common human experience. We may then examine its illusional nature — how it is used to sustain meaning — without surrendering to the casual assumption that it is delusional. As Hay remarks:

I doubt very much that religion is about to die out. The awareness out of which it grows is too widespread for that. More dangerous, because more likely, is that it may continue to be isolated from the mainstream of modern life. Human realities which are resolutely ignored tend, as Freud pointed out, to return in bizarre and fanatical forms. [Hay 1982, 212]

A further point relates to the psychodynamic assumptions with which common human experience is now approached. When we regard religion and its associated behaviour as illusory in character, we can then open up a way of thinking which takes account of psychological and analytical ideas and stances without locking ourselves into the associated nineteenth-century world-views, which are inevitably being increasingly discounted in the late twentieth century.

In summary, therefore, we can make progress with the questions of religious belief and common human experience if:

1. We recognize that religious experience by itself is not the central datum for trying to think about God when we take seriously the context of our experience as human beings. It is not an unimportant factor, but it is not self-evidently the one to which we should instinctively turn when questions of religion are raised.

2. We realize that, if we are to employ experience as a datum, this has to be common human experience. But without an interpretative model, that phenomenon remains unmanageable and incomprehensible.

3. We free illusion from the pejorative overtones and assumptions associated with delusion, and from the common-sense response that these terms refer only to evanescent ideas and are therefore unusable when we think theologically. By contrast, we shall see that taking illusion seriously can be a means by which in the late twentieth century we can continue to speak coherently of God.

The Importance of Illusion

When we discard the immediate application of the idea of

delusion to religion, we should be careful not to lose illusion. Illusion is a primary means by which we involve ourselves in our world. Winnicott demonstrated this in his experimental studies on childhood experience. He grasped the obvious, but profound, point that we can never speak only in terms of inter-personal relationships or about an individual's inner world. Reality is more complex, and in thinking about it we have to take into account both the reality of our inner selves and the fact of the external world. Both contribute to 'experience', so that the process of experiencing lies in an intermediate area, which is neither our inner world nor our outer world alone, but which includes both [Davis & Wallbridge 1981].

Earliest infancy offers an illustration of this. Every mother knows, and others can observe, that feeding involves an infinitely subtle series of actions. It is not just a functional matter of baby's need and mother's supply, but a complex mix of feelings and instinctual behaviour. If the mother seems to know when the child needs feeding and she responds, we have a well-fed baby and a confidently competent mother. The resulting aura of well-being also contributes to other aspects of the life of the pair and of the family in general. The interaction generates the experience which belongs to neither but only to both. When the mother offers her breast or bottle to the baby at the precise moment when the child has created inside itself its corresponding illusion of it, illusion is transformed into experience. Out of need, or perhaps even love, the child repeatedly creates from within itself a notion of the breast; mother provides the actual breast at the right moment; and so the child's illusion and the mother's reality combine and the experience coalesces.

This illustration further helps us distinguish between illusion and delusion. The area of experiencing is both where illusions are generated and where they perform their vital function. They become delusions if they are shifted out of this intermediate area, into either a person's inner or outer world alone. Both are equally unreal as the locus of experience. Psychotic delusion results when a person's imagination becomes so disordered that his relation to reality about himself and his world fragments.

Seen in this light, illusion is not a weakness or failure, nor does it compensate for some deficiency. It is neither an hallucination nor a wish-fulfilment. Indeed illusion is better thought of as a process. This becomes clear when we revert to the example of mother and baby. If at the start of the baby's life the mother is alert to her child's needs and responds to them as best she can, she fosters in the infant the illusion that her breast is almost part of him. He reaches for it and grasps it much as he explores his fingers or toes—it is practically an extension of himself. Eventually disillusion sets in as the baby grows and the mother becomes increasingly perceived as a separate, other person. But if there has not first been the initial opportunity for the illusion, progress towards maturity is likely to be hindered.

Illusion, therefore, is integral to what we call 'experience'. Although this example is taken from our earliest childhood, the interaction between inner reality and outer world, which creates experience, continues throughout our life. Just as a child needs illusion in order to develop, so throughout our life we have to create or find the opportunity to express and explore our illusions. Winnicott observes:

> I am, therefore, studying the substance of *illusion*, that which is allowed to the infant, and which in adult life is inherent in art and religion, and yet becomes the hallmark of madness when an adult puts too powerful a claim on the credulity of others, forcing them to acknowledge a sharing of illusion that is not their own. [Winnicott 1951, 230]

Illusion is a major dimension of life and me with which religion is concerned. For the pastor as theologian, therefore, claims about God and his dealings with mankind must be interpretable with respect to this area of human life and behaviour. They cannot, therefore, be confined to rational thought and discussion alone. For all the difficulty this idea engenders, God's dealings with his creation must include our unconscious world and those aspects of our behaviour which we tend to dismiss as irrational.

God as a Transitional Object

The non-technical concept of illusions suggests that they arise within our imagination. The art of the illusionist, for example, is to make our imaginations function in a restricted fashion so that he can manipulate them. In this discussion, however, the word is used in a more precise sense to refer to that experiencing which occurs neither solely inside nor solely outside the individual, but simultaneously both inside and outside, and in the interaction between the two. Inner reality and external life together create a space for this to occur.

This, too, is the area where transitional objects are located. This is a second key notion for our argument. The phrase also comes from Winnicott's work, but the phenomenon is one with which most people are familiar. Parents know the power of an irreplaceable piece of old, smelly cloth, without which a child will not sleep, or a teddy bear, for which no better or more worthy beast can substitute. The objects persist in improbable importance, carrying a significance which an observer simply cannot see. They mean more than they really are; yet they are real, tangible things. The object 'comes from without from one point of view, but not so from the point of view of the baby. Neither does it come from within; it is not an hallucination' [Winnicott 1951, 238].

This idea should not be too difficult for religious people. We are accustomed to thinking of God as at the same moment both transcendent and immanent, both beyond and yet within. We are also familiar with the way that belief in God does not so much get forgotten as relegated to limbo, only to resurface at critical moments in people's lives—what is often called 'folk religion'. The phrases 'persistent importance' and 'significance' are often used about religion and God. We have already noted how, in spite of expectations to the contrary, religion seems to persist as a complex phenomenon which cannot be isolated and dealt with in a special area called 'religious experience'. It is significant only in the realm of common human experience. These are precisely the ideas which Winnicott addresses in terms of our primary human experiences of birth and early development with his notion of transitional objects. It also seems likely, therefore, that ideas of God and religion are connected with them. This notion releases us from the over-simplified dualisms of both Freudian psychology and Christian theologies. We can now acknowledge and address the inexhaustible complexities of human behaviour and of God with which the pastor is daily confronted. Where does the sense of God originate? And, what is more, why, in spite of attempts to get rid of it, does it persist, to the discomfort not least of those who find themselves believing almost against their will?

One analytic study has vigorously pressed these questions. Anna-Maria Rizzuto has described case studies of four of her patients who held firm religious beliefs. She did not assume that these were delusions which required therapy, but considered them as part of the ordering structures of the individual's life. As a result, she concluded that our idea of God may be thought of as a special type of transitional object [Rizzuto 1979]. The space which such objects occupy is likely to be populated with any number of them. In the case of a child, for example, we notice the most obvious — perhaps the teddy bear — but this does not mean that it is necessarily the sole transitional object. Among the many available to us, that which we call 'God' turns out to possess a unique quality. Transitional objects are usually relegated to limbo as the individual grows and leaves them behind. There is rarely a conscious decision to reject them, but their use declines and they go out of existence as their function is no longer localized but is spread over the whole field of life. By contrast, however, 'God' seems to do the opposite: he drifts in and out of people's lives throughout their lifetime, and remains a particular object, not a diffuse idea. Among adolescents, for example, a sense of God may become alive as a factor during their development into adulthood. Whether eagerly embraced or vehemently dismissed, this particular transitional object takes on a vital function. For many (possibly most) people the process of creating and finding God never ceases.

Rizzuto, using Winnicott's ideas, concludes that the idea of the living God profoundly affects our sense of ourselves. Unlike most transitional objects, which tend to be ephemeral, he remains alive. God cannot be easily dismissed: 'Most of the time he shares the unpredictable life of the small child's teddy bear; when needed he is hurriedly pulled from his resting place, hugged or mistreated, and when the storm is over, neglectfully left wherever he may happen to be' [Rizzuto 1979, 203].

It may seem incongruous, even blasphemous, to compare God with a teddy bear. But this exactly describes the experience that pastors report in their dealings with people.

God is from time to time dragged from somewhere and brought to the pastor for recognition and action. In this framework, however, 'teddy bears' are not just children's toys, but are part of the illusory (and emphatically not delusory) material which we employ as we grow and which we continue to use in our adult life. As Winnicott further remarks: 'The transitional object is never under magical control like the internal object, nor is it outside control as the real mother is' [Winnicott 1951, 237]. The child's ability to create an illusion suggests to us omnipotence. The reality of the mother reminds us of limitations. Between them is the area of 'experiencing'. 'It is an area that is not challenged, because no claim is made on its behalf except that it shall exist as a resting-place for the individual engaged in the perpetual human task of keeping inner and outer reality separate yet interrelated' [Winnicott 1951, 230].

The description of transitional objects, their place and function, illuminates that area of our life where religion still flourishes. Rizzuto's specific study of the place of God in the lives of four patients confirms the distinctive nature and function of that particular transitional object. Although we unconsciously construct such objects simultaneously outside, inside and at the boundary of the self, there is also an actual bear.

Conclusion

Theologians and pastors need not become anxious when religion and God are discussed as illusions. Such terminology does not imply a pejorative dismissal of religion, but furnishes a description which regards it as integral to basic human experience. When we appreciate the significance of transitional objects for human life in general, religious belief and behaviour cannot be dismissed but have to be affirmed. And it certainly does not follow that maturity implies that religion is only for the immature or undeveloped. Our illustrations have been taken from infancy and early childhood because that is where the behaviour is clearly seen. But illusion contributes throughout life to what makes us who we are. We do not grow steadily along a continuum from the cradle to the grave, so that as we reach each new stage we leave the previous one behind. Nor is life cyclical, so that we are condemned to keep returning to our infancy in order each time to try and progress more satisfactorily.

The most appropriate picture of living is of a spiral of regression[1] and progression. The child remains in each of us, and from time to time throughout our adult life we move to and from that phase. Sometimes we may appear merely to return to a point that we, or others, have previously attained. But like the spiral, although we may have on one plane come back to where we were, on another we are at a new level. The description of religious behaviour as merely infantile, with the assumed consequence that it can be dismissed by those who are adults or mature, therefore needs careful examination. For religious belief and commitment may represent not escapism by reversion to a childhood state, but a valuable and creative regression, of importance both to individuals and to the society or communities of which they are citizens or members.

Ministers need not fear psychological approaches, but neither can they remain neutral about or indifferent to them. With our fellow men and women, we inhabit an everyday world which is widely influenced by simple and simplified psychological notions. There is nothing more familiar than mothers, babies and teddy bears. Our theological stance, then, has to be able to develop within this framework of understanding, and with some grasp of what such behaviour may signify, not only for people but also for our understanding of God. Freed from the confusion between delusion and illusion, which has bedevilled the dialogue between psychology and religion, and able to take up a psychodynamic basis for our sense of God, we can then attempt a practical, theologically based and psychologically informed ministry.

Note

1 'Regression' is a technical term, the importance of which will emerge in chapter 14. For a brief definition, see page 38.

THREE

The Perpetual Orphic Song: Assembling the Tools

Language is a perpetual Orphic song,
Which rules with Daedal harmony a throng
Of thoughts and forms, which else senseless and
shapeless were.

(Shelley, *Prometheus Unbound*)

To create a model by which to study how God encounters us at levels of our lives to which we have hitherto been less alert than we now are, we need tools. But to speak about aspects of the self and how God interacts with them, we need less a technical vocabulary—easily available dictionaries include Rycroft (1968) and Laplanche and Pontalis (1973)—than an agreed way of talking.

The Church has been rent by theological dispute and difference over words and language. Of all people, therefore, Christians should be among the most understanding when they survey the field of psychoanalytical study since Freud. Wherever we look we find difference, dispute and frequently acrimony. But through the smoke of controversy we can discern a basic thrust in the discipline and, more important for our purposes, clarify three fundamental concepts. A great deal of evidence points to these, and there is widespread agreement about them. They are: unconscious activity, transference (along with its corollary countertransference), and projection. These are large concepts which, however, provide tools with which to explore our human life and behaviour. Some appreciation of each is therefore essential for our enterprise. We shall briefly consider each in outline. This chapter may also be a useful reference point for ministers who are less familiar with this way of examining experience and theological understanding.

Unconscious Activity

Neither Freud nor his successors discovered unconscious activity. The study of human psychology predates its modern blossomings; dreams and the imagination have long, possibly always, been interpreted—usually by priests or prophets. The notion, however, that this dimension of human life is not merely to be noted but may also be systematically explored underlies much contemporary thought. Controversy about what precisely is being identified and examined continues, but for our purposes it is enough to recognize that there is such an area and that it can be examined. We cannot in our theological thinking retreat from this new terrain, even though we may scarcely have begun its exploration.

'Unconscious' may be either a noun or an adjective. It describes processes which are not conscious. But that is a very large field. Today it is widely and casually used as a noun—'the unconscious'. Freud [1915] employs this to refer to part of the system where in his view of psychic structure primary processes, that is, those on which we do not reflect and of which we are scarcely aware, operate. That is why he called dreams 'the royal road to the unconscious' [Freud 1900]. We need not, however, in the light of subsequent developments, resort to the idea of an entity within us called 'the unconscious'. We may better think of ourselves as 'people who think, imagine, feel and act, sometimes consciously, sometimes unconsciously' [Rycroft 1985, 26]. The contrast is not between, on the one hand, behaviour of which we are consciously aware and which appears in the guise of our more rational decisions and, on the other, unconscious activity which emerges as irrational behaviour. On the contrary, we now recognize that human beings have a way of being which is not always conscious, although in some circumstances it can be brought to consciousness. It sometimes may disclose itself in pathological behaviour which requires treatment. This connection is especially strong in the popular view of the unconscious world, because it was through the treatment of disturbed patients that Freud originally discovered the 'talking cure' and came to recognize the unconscious dimension to the behaviour of us all.

Unconscious activity is as important a factor in our everyday life as conscious reflection. It is best thought of as the sum of dynamic elements that make up our personality. But because unconscious activity is a different sort of process from that of conscious activity, we cannot be aware of all these elements. From time to time, however, some may be brought to our attention. We may, for example, not follow Freud in his view of dreams. But from the experience of dreaming we can be aware that there are processes within us which relate to who we are but which are qualitatively different from those by which we deliberately choose to live. It is that area of life, however we interpret it and become aware of its existence, which is called unconscious.

In today's world it is not only significant because of its intrinsic importance. The idea is so widespread — even though not always understood and frequently miscalled 'the sub-conscious' — that it is difficult, if not impossible, to live in the contemporary world, either at the level of common human experience or in the prevailing intellectual climate, without being prepared to take this dimension into account.

One major development in thinking about unconscious activity has been an increasing grasp of the significance of relationships and interrelationships. Winnicott, whose work with children I have already mentioned, frequently emphasized that, whenever a child was presented to him, he never in his framework of thinking saw solely a child; there was always the child/mother relationship to consider. This emphasis on relationship reminds us that unconscious processes are not private, arising from within an isolated individual. They are part of the self which grows from and through relationship. It is appropriate, therefore, to offer as an example of how such processes can be disclosed for examination, a group of people and its unconsciously motivated behaviour rather than an individual.

Eight people in a church study group were discussing belief in the resurrection. They were not finding it easy, as they questioned their beliefs and found passages of the Gospels obscure. The name of David Jenkins, the Bishop of Durham, was introduced, it seemed almost casually. As one, the group began to indulge in anti-intellectual and anti-episcopal argument and cohered. Each member appeared to feel better, being let off the hook of their own questions and of having to examine themselves. On another occasion the same group faced another controversial topic. This time they sat around telling stories and exchanging anecdotes; some arrived late; coffee took an interminable time to make and serve; and the evening evaporated in chit-chat.

The way that this group behaved on each occasion illustrates conscious and unconscious behaviour. At a conscious level the members assembled to study and learn; they took that decision and attended. Unconsciously, however, there were other purposes of which they were not immediately aware, but which emerged in different ways. In this instance the unconscious life of the group seems to have been designed to defend the members against any learning which might change them and their beliefs. First they attacked a notional enemy, who was not, of course, really opposed to them. They were never likely to be involved directly with the Bishop of Durham, and accordingly he was unreal as someone with whom to engage. On the second occasion they colluded in elevating trivial things and activities so as to allow them to escape the stress of beginning study. The precise dynamics of this group are unimportant for present purposes; we need simply to note conscious and unconscious behaviour.

Recognition of the dimension of unconscious behaviour is crucial for our contemporary estimates of people, both as individuals or in groups. The arguments about whether it is locatable in 'the unconscious' should not obscure the key issue: it is a recognizable dimension of our human existence, and any gospel for today must include reflection on how God might address this facet of ourselves. This is even more necessary when that gospel is proclaimed by men and women who offer a pastoral ministry, which is informed by awareness of unconscious influences in human life.

Transference

The second major tool for our study is closely linked with unconscious activity — transference and its complement, countertransference. 'Transference' is occasionally used in a general sense, but on the whole it remains a distinctively psychoanalytic idea. It refers to the process by which the unconscious wishes of the patient are made accessible, so that they can be identified and interpreted. In the specific setting of psychoanalysis, the analyst becomes the focus for the patient's transference, which he encourages, tolerates and interprets. Patients may thus live through experiences that they have had with other people, chiefly members of their family [Freud 1910]. The analyst, within the secure setting of the treatment, is available for use. Although a popular image of this process is that the analyst 'becomes', say, the father, we should note that people do not through this process relive actual experiences. The manifestations of transference are not straightforward repetitions, but are instances of deep unconscious wishes.

How transference functions and how exactly it should be understood remain disputed. But, as with the concept of unconscious behaviour, there is little doubt about the process. It generates a relationship in which feelings (such as love, hate and resentment) are felt more powerfully than the actual situation demands. The patient, for example, does not in 'real' terms love or hate the analyst. But in the dynamic setting between them he may experience such emotions. As these are allowed—even encouraged—and interpreted, hitherto obscure processes underlying a person's life may be revealed and addressed. In transference, the patient 'transfers' on to the analyst feelings and attitudes derived from childhood relationships.

There are obviously some technical problems with such a notion. But these do not immediately affect the basic insight and its importance for pastoring. For we are not concerned with the specific content and detail of transference so much as with the fact of the process. This is not confined to the analytic situation. The concept of transference, like that of unconscious activity, takes us into the heart of everyday human life—our relationships with one another—and consequently into questions about who we ourselves are. It is a central insight for contemporary life, and, as will appear, for theology and pastoral practice.

Ferenczi, an early associate of Freud, soon recognized that it had a much wider application [Ferenczi 1916], and Freud himself acknowledged the same point: '[Transference] is a universal phenomenon of the human mind . . . and in fact dominates the whole of each person's relations to his human environment' [Freud 1925].

This is, therefore, a dimension to human affairs to which the pastor needs to attend. It is about using and being used. The clearest examples of transference come from neurotic patients in treatment. For example, it is not unusual for the inevitable break in treatment which occurs when the analyst goes on holiday to stir up new dimensions in the transference. One patient dreamt powerfully of the absent analyst, while she angrily determined never to return to him again since he had let her down. Following this through, she discovered aspects of a missing relationship with her parents which had been affecting her life without her realizing it. But this sort of activity is not confined to technical analysis. All of us are in some way caught up in such behaviour, and not least, when speaking of 'being used', the minister.

For pastors, without the defensive security of a contract— time, place and payment—the complementary notion of countertransference is especially important. This acknowledges that any relationship, however professional, is between two feeling human beings. Analysts have sometimes been pictured as blank screens on to which patients draw their own fantasies, or as unresponding receptacles for whatever the patient may wish to dispose of. Yet this image is clearly deficient. When people meet, whatever the formal structure of their relationship, feelings are reciprocal. The term 'counter-transference' describes the feeling response of a person who is the focus for transference.

Countertransference is also universal. Because everyday pastoral encounters with common human experience are less structured than the meeting of an analyst with a patient, there is more space for unaddressed transference on the part of the person approaching the minister and for unrecognized countertransference in return. For the pastor, as will become clearer later, awareness of this is especially important. In the informal setting of most of their ministry, it is the means of entry to the dynamic world in which they are working. 'What is happening to me?' is a better ministerial question than 'What is the matter with him?' Every encounter which he or she has with individuals or with groups contains this element. If we are aware that people are using us in some fashion, then we need also to be aware that to some extent we too are using them in a complementary fashion. The professional question is how such feelings are recognized, acknowledged, handled and used.

Transference and countertransference are not remote, theoretical ideas. They describe fundamental human behaviour that occurs both between individuals and within groups. Some grasp of it, therefore, provides a valuable resource in the day-to-day work of ministry. But there is also the theological question. When we consider how God engages with our unconscious aspects, we shall have to take into account transference.

Projection

The third key notion is 'projection'. This is also a process with which most people are familiar, even if the term is not used. Transference involves a repetition of the past by inappropriately imposing an aspect of that past on something or someone in the present, as, for instance, in the relationship between patient and analyst. It also, however, arises spontaneously in human relationships. Projection is similarly a universal phenomenon, but it is always a facet of present behaviour. The term describes the way in which we escape from ourselves into other people. This usually involves disowning an aspect of ourselves that we wish to deny or refuse to face by locating it in another person and dealing with it there. For example, we may believe that someone is behaving towards us in a hostile fashion and feel cowed by this. But in our relationship with them, their apparent hostility may in fact represent an aggressiveness that we are unable or unwilling to recognize in ourselves. As a result they may feel full of emotions that they cannot identify as belonging to them. This experience is both mystifying and incapacitating for them, but can be, at least temporarily, freeing for us. Essentially, therefore, we use projection to protect ourselves from ourselves.

As with the other processes that we have looked at, projection is not solely an individual form of behaviour. It is also a characteristic of groups. Indeed, as a phenomenon it is sometimes more easily discerned in a group or an organization.

For example, in a hospital powerful emotions are stirred up. Sickness and death and the complex series of roles that people hold generate powerful but disturbingly intimate emotions. As a result, different groups, which have legitimate functions in the treatment programme, may become identified and used for other covert purposes. Nurses, for instance, have a vital function along with doctors in providing care and treatment. But doctors may not wish to acknowledge the messiness of patient care, and so leave this to the nurses. This can be claimed to be legitimate; it is 'nurses' work'. But it may also be a way of disowning parts of the doctors' responsibilities that they do not wish to face. Thus different individuals or groups of people are relied on to hold feelings, which are thus redistributed within the setting of everyday working. This may relieve one set of people in the organization, but in another group it produces an uncomfortable sense that something is wrong, although people are unsure what [Shapiro & Carr 1987].

Ministers will be familiar with similar phenomena in churches. A verger or an organist may seem to be filled with strong feelings, the origins of which he cannot identify and which he can express only in an angry outburst. The reason may be that the minister and/or the congregation are projecting into people whose views (it is believed) can be disregarded stresses and feelings which are arising from the church's activities. In ecclesiastical folklore, organists and vergers are often characterized as temperamental and 'difficult' people. When they leave, however, the episode is 'understood' in terms of their personality and presumed inability to get on with others.

This phenomenon of individual and corporate projection has become a more prominent idea as thinking has moved away from an earlier preoccupation with instincts, towards our modern awareness of relationships. All relationships are to some degree projective. Such projection is often considered something to be discerned and dealt with, so as to help an individual towards maturity, or, in the case of a group or members of an organization, to more purposeful and effective work. This is not a wholly unsound approach, but it is also important to perceive that, like unconscious activity and transference, projection is a basic, or given, form of normal human behaviour. If it is appreciated as such, it can become creative for all concerned.

The pastor who wishes to be effective needs to be alive to projective behaviour. A public role such as his is liable to be a focus for others to project aspects of themselves into him. But ministers also need to reflect on what they may inadvertently be projecting into others. Again though, as with the other terms that we have examined, ministers also require a theological interpretation of the place of projection in the way God engages with our human life at its unconscious level.

Conclusion

These three insights — unconscious process, transference and projection — undergird contemporary thinking about human behaviour, both individual and corporate. There is no agreement about the precise interpretation of any of them, yet there is widespread agreement that they are significant. For our purposes, we can now see that, although the field is fraught with problems and disputes, there is no intrinsic hostility between analytically informed thinking, upon which both sophisticated and popular views of contemporary common human experience depend, and theological interpretation. Either religion is concerned with these central aspects of human life and development or it is irrelevant. God, likewise, must be interpretable in some fashion in this specific world, or the pastor and theologian eventually loses touch with contemporary men and women.

FOUR

Discordant Elements in One Society: Individual Experience in its Social Context

---

Dust as we are, the immortal spirit grows
Like harmony in music; there is a dark
Inscrutable workmanship that reconciles
Discordant elements, makes them cling together
In one society.

(Wordsworth, *The Prelude*)

The three concepts of unconscious activity, transference and projection are not only valuable tools for interpreting individual behaviour; they also clarify how people relate to one another, particularly in institutions. In order to use them in our theological and pastoral reflection, we need to employ them in our thinking about churches. This is more demanding than might at first appear. Freud, for example, became confused here. Falling back upon non-analytic concepts, although under the guise of using them, he produced a confused and confusing set of ideas about religion, which still influence some [Badcock 1980]. They have also contributed to the unnecessary divide between theologians and practitioners of other behavioural disciplines.

The Group Effect

The core issue for working ministers is the human behaviour with which they continually deal in the light of what they find that they can say about God. Common human experience is composed of relationships and interactions. These are as much between the individual's inner and outer worlds as between separate people and groups. Religious experience is

35

no exception to this. It is not a private area of an individual's internal world. Questions of relationship are more significant between religious people and others than among associations of like-minded believers. Even the most intensely personal religious experience has its shared dimension. This may be seen in people's association with one another in their membership of a church. But those who have nothing directly to do with churches also give their experience some shape by so dissociating.

There is no such person as the complete isolate. Although a hermit might seem an example, even he is a function of his world in the sense that his behaviour has to some extent been conditioned by it. He renounces society *because* he is involved in it and chooses to act in a distinctive fashion. Similarly, interactions with others affect our lives, even when no group is physically present. Our notions of groups influence our behaviour. Our religious affiliation ('Church of England', 'Jewish'), our nationality (leading to our self-awareness as 'citizen') and our other associations (clubs, schools, societies) all affect our estimate of ourselves and others' perceptions of us. We are, in a sense, permanently in groups. To take a specific instance: a factory worker is not just influenced by his colleagues on the site. His home life comes with him, and his sense of the general impact of 'the company', which employs him, to a degree determines his behaviour.

Any model for linking pastoral activity and theological reflection through common human experience must incorporate this vision. Although a pastoral encounter may look like the meeting of two individuals, each represents and is involved in a wide range of groupings which affect that encounter. This dimension has been increasingly recognized in pastoral training. But in general, although useful sociological insights have been offered, means have not on the whole been developed which pastors might work with them in their dealings with individuals and groups, outside and inside the Church. One reason for this is the difficulty involved in matching the discoveries about individual psychology with insights derived from attempts to interpret people in their social context.

In the previous chapter we used a couple of organizational instances to illuminate the idea of unconscious activity and projection. We all live with our conscious and unconscious selves; similarly, a group can be seen as operating on two levels. One, which matches our conscious mind, is the level of its work — what the group exists to achieve. The other, which is like our unconscious selves, consists of powerful emotional behaviour, which frequently appears to be irrational. Most pastors in practice work with large and small groups, at least as often as (if not more frequently than) they work with individuals. Any perspective on ministry must therefore provide coherence between the way we regard individuals and the way we perceive groups. There is also the theological question. Since religious experience is part of common human experience, it is not private: it has a social or corporate aspect, a dimension which is not confined to association with like-minded believers. It is included in everyday life in community, and within a total world with which God is believed in some way to engage. Pastors therefore have no choice but to attend to the group aspect of interpreting human experience.

This recognition brings with it another advantage. Although the insights of psychoanalysts and psychologists are not divorced from the activity of anyone who works with people, they are nevertheless expressed in technical language. The problem can occur that some pastors, in acquiring the insights (and consequently the language) of these disciplines, also drift into the assumption that their ministry is located in the same field, considering it as therapeutic rather than (as we shall see) teaching or educational. But thinking about human behaviour in language which is used about groups is a helpful bulwark against such a shift. It tends to employ more familiar terms and so appear less dauntingly technical. These advantages may encourage casual thinking, but the risk is worthwhile. For the advantage is that this easier language enables ministers to note and discuss the significance of unconscious processes for pastoral ministry and theological understanding in terms which are more immediately accessible than their psychoanalytic correlates.

The Dynamics of Groups

W. R. Bion's seminal work integrated thinking about the

individual's unconscious behaviour with that of the group [Bion 1961; Rioch 1975; Brown 1985]. He was working as a therapist with groups of patients, when he noticed that there was a group dimension to what was happening. This was more than the sum of individual disturbances; it appeared to be something 'extra'. The group took on a perceptible life of its own, and the members interacted not only with each other but also with this larger life. Further study demonstrated that just as the individual has a conscious and unconscious life, so a group had its work (its conscious dimension, or task) and underlying behaviour (its unconscious, or what Bion called its 'basic assumption', life).

He discerned three of these 'basic assumptions'. Although refinements have since been made, they remain fundamental, because they represent three facets of individual development on the larger canvas of group life: dependence, pairing, and fight/flight.

A group caught up in *dependence* behaves as if it has met to sustain someone as its leader, protector and provider and so release itself from work. This person is believed to be omniscient and omnicompetent, and to be able to do all that is demanded of him. Dependence is a familiar characteristic of individual behaviour. Our initial reliance upon our mother continues through maturity, as we have already noted. But if we are not to be stuck in a permanent state of idealizing our mother—stultifying immature dependence—we have to acknowledge that our dependence remains real.

Some groups are marked by unexamined optimism, as if they have met to create a sign of hope and affirm it. They manifest *pairing*. To produce the sign of hope, a Messiah or saviour figure, the group unconsciously elects a pair and lets them get on with the work. The atmosphere is suffused with hopefulness, whether for a new leader or a new world. But this is clearly an unconscious assumption, since the longed-for world or leader is never allowed to come into being. If this were to happen, the group would be shifted from the reassurance of its hope to having to do something with what it has created. The basis of this assumption in individual development is observed when people rely on each other in relationships. Passion and mutuality, rivalry and competition all play critical roles in the development of a mature person.

In a sense this is the most primitive of the basic assumptions, representing the biological urge to procreate and assure a future for the race.

A third type of group feels the pressure for action, either to get on with it or avoid it. But whichever of these two modes is operating, the basic attitude of this group—the third assumption of *fight/flight*— is active. This, unlike the other two, has a thrust in two directions and so is unstable and ambivalent, as capable of crazy fighting as of headlong flight, and sometimes switching from one to the other with bewildering speed. Fight/flight, this double dynamic, relates to an early phase of individual growth, when the child affirms himself both by aggressive assertion and by defensive self-protection. Probably the most fragile area for both the individual and the group, this dynamic has to be harnessed if we are to achieve anything.

This framework for interpreting group life is useful for handling common human experience, both as an ingredient in theological reflection and as the basic material of pastoral ministry. By thus linking the individual and the group, we can now begin to think of human beings without the constricting recourse to personal psychology alone. Similarly, this approach allows us to take seriously the social dimension of our lives without discounting individuality. This is a coherent ground on which to interpret common human experience. In using this approach, we have to deal *at the same time* with personal claims to specific experience and the group or social manifestations of it. Our large and vastly incomprehensible emotions—fear, love, anxiety, hope, joy, and so on—become amenable to study without the risk of their being, or seeming to be, explained away. The same is true of religious experience as a facet of this common human experience.

Pastors, Individuals and Groups

'The individual is the creature of the group, the group of the individual' [Miller & Rice 1967, 17]. This perception follows when we bring individual life and corporate association under the one model of interpretation. But to assign the group such a place in thinking about the individual runs counter to many contemporary assumptions. Yet by so doing we can pay due attention to the social and cultural factors which shape common human experience. We are becoming increasingly sensitive to how such factors determine the shape of Christian faith and practice, theology and pastoral strategy. Experience is not like putty, malleable and vulnerable to any outside pressure. It is a process, or a series of *inter*actions, taking place between complex facets, conscious and unconscious, of the self and its environment (the inner and outer worlds), and individuals and groups.

When, however, as pastors we include this perspective in our thinking, it creates a problem: it removes a major defence — our limited professional view of ourselves. We customarily use this as a filter to restrict the range of data that we wish to accept as relevant to us as ministers. Any set of people, including pastors, is likely to find itself in the same position as did these social workers. A report describes what happened to trainees who began to think simultaneously of *both* the individual *and* the corporate dimensions to themselves and their roles:

> Areas of concern were raised . . . around the question of where and how the boundary of professional intervention could be defined once the individual as the primary focus for attention was abandoned. One despairing respondent commented on the flexibility and confusion engendered as part of the process of taking [this type of] thinking on board and felt that what was involved was a wish to do 'world therapy'. [Gorell Barnes 1984, 27]

Thinking in this way may appear to complicate everyday concerns which previously demanded only practical responses. The result is that we may feel that we should limit ourselves to description alone and abandon any attempt at evaluation and interpretation. 'World therapy' — getting everything in order before we attempt anything — is not an option for working pastors; it seems better not to know too much.

But while the approach commended here is based on acquiring, assessing and reflecting on evidence, it does not imply that this is an end in itself. It is offered in order to assist those who are already ministering (often to more effect than they know) to develop their activity for God, for others and for themselves. Its usefulness, therefore, to our pastoral-theological enterprise is tested by the extent to which it has the following two effects. It must, on the one hand, illuminate the interpretations of the Christian tradition which we have received and which are the source and ground of faith, enabling us to think about them in intimate connection with common human experience. (Christianity is about salvation, and unless Christian belief demonstrates an observable effect, the detailed content of theology is scarcely important.) On the other hand, if this way of thinking is theologically valuable, it must also facilitate a closer relationship between two major branches of theology — systematic and applied. This is one of the painful areas of the contemporary divide between theology and pastoring. The problem is not how pastoring can be better informed by systematic theology, but also how the work of the theologian can be further integrated with present-day experience of Christian people and their contemporaries.

Current discussion about and influential theologies of the Church show us why we have to address this question. Amid the invigorating discussions and often convincing arguments one factor disappears — the *actual* forms that Christian belief and activity *at present* take. For example, novel work is being done by theologians who take praxis as their theological base. (We do not have to look to the South American churches, in a culture which is alien to ours; praxis has also been applied to thinking about Western churches [Metz 1981].) These theologians often try to work practically with churches and with other people of goodwill. But when they begin to draw implications for church life in the social and political area, they tend to lose sight of the ways in which existing believers and worshipping congregations express their Christian faith. The question of whether contemporary — no doubt in many ways degenerate — forms of the Church have any positive theological significance seems not to be asked. They are acute on what (in their view and as a consequence of their theological perceptions) the Church *ought* to be. But they do not offer much guidance on how it might become like this, starting from its current shape and who constitutes its present membership [Moltmann 1977].

Yet every pastor, whatever his theological and political attitude, knows that the reality of the Church is as it is. What is more, where faith and religion are concerned, any idea of clearing a field by abandoning the past is futile. Interpretations of Christian faith in contemporary terms must include an adequate account both of churches as they are as well as of the present-day experiences of believers and others to which they contribute.

The approach proposed here is offered for use as a way of interpreting common human experience. It invites pastors, who are already caught up in present realities, however much these may justly be under theological censure, to take them as their primary data in the Christian theological enterprise. Ultimately there is only one genuine point of testing: To what extent does it provide and foster a practical theology?

Summary of Part One:
The Argument to this Point

We have prepared the way towards trying to integrate our reflections on pastoral practice, theology and Christian discipleship. This discussion has inevitably ranged widely and covered areas of thought which may have been unfamiliar to many ministers. It may therefore be useful to summarize them.

Religious experience is a vital datum in any theological enterprise, but especially in one designed to link pastoral practice and theological thinking. It is a facet of common human experience, occupying a particular, though not unique, area of human life, where transitional phenomena are located. God, when thought of from this perspective, occupies space within, outside and at the boundary of the individual. This transitional object, 'God', provides the model for the sense of God with which people commonly live and work, which they accept and reject, develop and dismiss. Although in religion, not least Christianity, God's Fatherhood is a prominent theme, this should not obscure the fact that our original modelling of God seems primarily to derive from child-mother relationships.

The concept of 'transitional object' is important for two reasons. First, it enables us to think about religious experience and faith in God in terms of our internal world without confining the idea of God to that area. Second, although the way in which we use these objects arises in our childhood, the pattern of behaviour which is connected with transitional objects persists throughout our adult life. This is again significant for the pastor, who not only encounters childlike behaviour in himself and those with whom he ministers, but who also spends much time dealing with adults and urging

43

mature behaviour upon people. Childlikeness, as the gospel also indicates, is one condition of maturity. We cannot enter the Kingdom of God unless we accept it like a child (Luke 17.15 – 18).

Religion in common human experience, however, is corporate. Individuals, sometimes alone and sometimes in groups, claim religious experience, but it does not arise in either one or the other. It is an outcome of an interaction between a religious group and its setting. We cannot sustain a discussion of religious experience which omits its social dimension. What is the significance for the believer of the fact and continuance of the belief in which he or she shares? This question faces him as a person. But the next one is about his effect on this belief: Where does the believer fit into and contribute to the network of religious belief which enables him to give his belief its particular shape and content? And how does this encourage him (by his believing) to create and modify it?

This is the question of participation, not merely at an intellectual level of saying the creeds or developing theological thought, but at the emotional level of generating something with and for others. It comes about as the believer participates in shared beliefs and by believing them also affects them. Every believer stands in a tradition or line of belief, and has in some way inherited it. But by his believing he also alters what he inherits for all with whom in the present he shares belief and for any who in the future will make that belief their own. The corporate aspects of belief, then, is not only about a group of people who happen to share a common attitude or creed. It represents part of the network which ensures that belief continues by critically engaging with it.

Accordingly, for his ministry the pastor needs a stance from which to interpret individual experience and group activity together, both theoretically and practically. Although, as with all theories, the outline given here has its limitations, it seems to offer a way by which to explore religious experience as a facet of common human experience. In our thinking on pastoral ministry, therefore, we can operate with the two chief foci of experience—the self and its human context— without devaluing or inadvertently diminishing either.

The skill of the pastor lies precisely here: How can he give full value to the individual who confronts him; acknowledge the significance of upbringing and other social contexts, including the immediate environments which that individual inhabits; and then interpret this in the context of the ultimate setting which he himself represents — God? A familiar enough daily issue for the pastor, this is now a crucial question for the credibility of Christian theology. The pastor whose work is not informed by a theology which is congruent with these questions is vulnerable. He may be pulled into some other form of work than Christian ministry, or he may succumb to presenting a dogmatically Christian self which is so defended against his own feelings that he will be unable to minister to others.

Any theological scheme must therefore give central attention to this question: What is it to speak of God from our Christian tradition in our individual and corporate human contexts as these are today understood?

In the light of contemporary thought about individuals and groups, there are factors that we have to take into account with which our predecessors did not have to deal. We are not in the business of supplanting an 'old' language with a so-called 'new' one, abandoning philosophy for psychology. Rather we are about to re-examine key parts of the inherited theological tradition, or basic doctrine, which forms the content and the process of Christian belief and practice in ministry.

PART TWO

Exploring the Issues

Introduction

In Part Two we shall consider three Christian classics. Each
section follows the same pattern:

1) a discussion about the connection between a major
facet of human behaviour (and its associated dynamic) and
the theological necessities of the classic;
2) a consideration of the reciprocal links between theology
and ministry, and the way that these illuminate each other
and the classic itself;
3) an exposition of the consequences of such thinking for
pastoral practice;
4) a discussion of a relevant facet of Christian discipleship.

The aim, therefore, is that theological undergirding,
ministerial practice and Christian discipleship might come
into critical and creative relations with each other.

The first classic considered, the incarnation, is the most
difficult, both in itself and in terms of its associated
behavioural dynamics. This is therefore the fullest and in
some ways the most complicated section, both as the reader's
first encounter with an unfamiliar way of thinking and
because of its content. It is not, however, essential that the
next three sections should be read in the order printed, and
the reader may find it easier to read the chapters in each
section in a different order, moving, for example, from facets
of discipleship to the discussion about human behaviour and
the doctrine.

A. Otherness Says 'I': The Classic of the Incarnation

———

Love's possibilities of realization
Require an Otherness that can say I.
        (W. H. Auden, *For the time being*)

FIVE

Incarnation, Limitation and Negotiation

Today's thinking about the incarnation displays the same concern with relationships that marks our contemporary world in general. They are researched and studied. Popular literature abounds on all aspects of human relating. In theological studies similar interest is shown. Maurice Wiles provides a typical example when he speaks of salvation as 'an unbreakable relationship of loving obedience to God for which the best (though still imperfect) analogy is that of personal relationship' [Wiles 1976, 108].

In everyday life people go to great lengths to find a loving relationship. They pay therapists and counsellors, the new priests of an undogmatic religion of personal attention [North 1972]. Yet in its pastoral ministry the Church does not seem able to use the opportunity of this ferment to make an effective link between such human relationships and the gospel interpretation of God's dealings with us. As a result it is in a bind: it speaks fluently of care and love, and tries in various ways to offer both, but it lacks a gospel, an effective message of changed life with God. Something feels missing as the Christian message becomes indistinguishable from other contemporary exhortations to care for a neighbour who may or may not need that concern. Opportunities for action multiply as horizons extend from Church, through parish and society, to nation and world. But a sense of guilt accompanies these efforts to offer care and love. The greater the need seems to be, the more it looks like evidence that we, the Christians who glibly speak of God's love and ours, have in practice proved insufficiently loving.

This preoccupation with relationships expresses a form of hope. The lonely individual or isolated community seeks a contact with someone else or another group through which they may find a sense of permanence in an unreliable world or temporary gratification in a joyless environment. The exact form is not for the moment important: it remains hope. Our biological motivation to reproduce underlies the feeling that, if only we can get together, things as yet unknown will be created. But relationships are more significant than this. The offspring produced are the next generation; but they are also continuing evidence of the relationship itself. They, therefore, carry the hopes in which the partners invest.

Hope in this sense arises because it is a function of relationship in a context—two people, two groups, two nations. In common human experience such hope is not merely an option; it is a fundamental component of living. Accounts from the Nazi extermination camps or about the survival of prisoners of conscience show this. Even the existentialist writers, for all their overwhelming sense of despair, confirm the significance of hope for our human existence. When our hoping part is removed (and this is itself notoriously difficult to achieve), the result is not diminished human life but a dehumanized existence, which scarcely qualifies to be called either 'human' or 'life'.

Relationships are focal points for others as well as for the partners. The stronger the sense of hope in a particular relationship, the more likely it is that the couple are expressing something on behalf of others. One obvious instance is marriage and the pressures on it today. These pressures do not arise solely from the high expectations which the partners may individually have of each other, but from the way that they also have to cope with anxieties which are endemic in our society. Economic problems, for example, which even governments seem unable to solve, are left to newly married couples to resolve. They have to earn enough to live on or manage the stresses brought about by unemployment, even if the nation cannot do so. And the pressure is increased by casual talk of the sanctity of marriage and the need for stable family life. Hope is thus invested in the couple which is greater than they can realize. We can now begin to appreciate why partnerships—good friends, parents and children, married couples, professional associations and even national alliances—are so fragile. Because both the partners and others invest in the hope, the disappointment and anger that results when that hope fails is out of proportion and so becomes bewildering and mystifying.

Any analogy which we may draw between salvation and human relating must therefore include a recognition of the way in which such a relationship enables life to be sustained by others as well as by those directly involved. The Christian minister is concerned in this way with relationships and hope. His ministry involves him with people who are already in complex ways, often hidden from him, interacting with each other. In his specifically religious activities, too, such as worship and prayer, he is establishing a connection or relationship between God and man or between this world and the next. People expect him to do this. Indeed, it is when the Church and its ministers are being most distinctively religious that their opportunities for general ministry seem to become most frequent and usable.

The Christian classic which connects with this dimension of human life is the incarnation. Often thought of in terms of identification—'God with us' or 'God as one of us'—we can better focus it as a series of different relationships, how they are generated and why they are sustained.

The Pairings in the Classic of the Incarnation

It scarcely needs stating that this doctrine is central to Christian belief. For some it is *the* Christian classic. The incarnation of Jesus Christ is a central theme of worship; theologians revert to it as a core problem of Christian theology; and whatever attempts are made to shift it from its central, but problematic, status, it persistently returns. There is no clear evidence that this state of affairs is changing or is about to change, in spite of flurries of argument, books and pamphlets. Current disputes echo ancient acrimonies. Anyone who wishes to face up to Christianity, whether as believer or interested inquirer, must still confront the classic of the incarnation.

So central a doctrine is bound to cause controversy, some of it seemingly remote from ordinary belief or the practice of everyday ministry. These disputes, however, all indicate one obvious point: wherever you turn in thinking about God incarnate, you come up against linking, or twoness. The language makes extensive use of 'and'—God *and* Christ; Father *and* Son; fully God *and* fully man; or, more philosophically, time *and* eternity; immanence *and* transcendence. The thrust of Chalcedon, and most subsequent theologies of the incarnation, was to preserve 'and'. Substitute 'or' for any one of those 'ands', and you were more likely than not to have become heretical. The four famous adverbs which refer to the union of the two natures sustain the point: 'unconfusedly, unchangeably, indivisibly, inseparably'.

God and Jesus Christ form a primary pair. The Gospels are unequivocal about this relationship: Jesus prays to and with God; and his disciples and others associate him with God as a prophet, a miracle-worker, or the Messiah. Whether or not this last was Jesus' own claim, the stories present a Jesus who was invited by both God and his fellow men and women to function on their behalf. Over the question of Messiahship, for example, he appears to have resisted the title. Maybe he feared misunderstanding. But perhaps, too, he was aware that the fantasy world which in common human experience is constructed around relationships is too fragile to be a means of salvation, however intensely all concerned may believe that it is. The contemporary expectation was that the link between God and the Messiah would instantly achieve the salvation of the people. So Jesus consistently reinterpreted the role of 'Messiah', allowing people to use the term but always giving it back in a changed version. The most notable instance is his response to Peter's confession. Peter cries out, 'You are the Messiah'. To which Jesus responds in terms of the suffering Son of Man (Mark 8.27ff). He thus resisted the natural, but deluded, investment in a pair for its own sake.

There are other pairs or twonesses: God and mankind and God and the world are linked through the incarnation. And there is further the partnership between the man Jesus and mankind in general. As John Robinson aptly describes it, from whichever angle we approach the incarnation, it is like trying to put two billiard balls on the same spot [Robinson 1973].

The pair of *God and man*, the central point of dispute around the formula of Chalcedon, became historically the test of orthodoxy. Today it is questioned anew, although not so much because of suspicion about the quality of the arguments. There seems little more to say about them. The problem now becomes acute in a different way. It arises because the concept of humanity, which is one pole of the union of God and man in Christ, has in our age become differently problematic. The Chalcedonian approach relies upon the human term in the pair remaining reliable and accessible; at least, we have reckoned, we know what we mean by 'man', even if 'God' remains more difficult. But the human sciences have removed such apparent certainty and have thus made this orthodoxy almost impossible for many.

The second paired relationship — *God and the world* — asks how there can be universal implications from any special divine activity. Providence and divine intervention are never easy ideas, but the problems they raise are felt with increased intensity in the pluralistic world which we now inhabit. The finality of Christ, the link between all religions and Christianity and between Christ and religious expression in non-Christian religions, all of which occur when we think of an incarnation, become points of renewed controversy.

The third link — that between *man and man* — points us to the relationship between Jesus and the individual. Here is the evangelical challenge that Christ lives and dies for each believer. Issues of Jesus' personal identity enlarge into questions about how Christ relates to the Church and of how Christians (and for that matter others) share in his continuing work. Spirituality and sacramental theology, as well as what it means to speak of 'knowing Christ', come into focus.

All of these pairings in the incarnation stir up for the Christian minister more than interesting and important questions about the content of his faith. However technical a discussion may be, the doctrine draws him to the hard issues of his everyday dealing with people — the nature of man; why relationships occur; and how hope is to be sustained. There are major issues of theology, the day-to-day business of pastoral ministry, and the substance of Christian spirituality and prayer. How we might hold these together in a coherent fashion is the point of the investigation that follows.

Relationship, Experience and Religious Experience

All attempts to suggest that the incarnation is of merely

historical or antiquarian interest appear to fail. Individuals from time to time may come to that conclusion for themselves, but affirmation of and controversy about the incarnation are as rife as ever. It does not go away. Belief in the incarnation demands that we grapple with difficulties. Although some resolve these dilemmas simplistically, most Christians seem willing to continue the struggle rather than to surrender the doctrine. Indeed some say that this exertion and conflict gives Christianity its identity [Sykes 1984]. But there is more to it than this. Running through Christian experience, in prayer, worship and what it feels like to call oneself 'Christian', is regard for Jesus as one to be venerated. This attitude was one mark of the emerging doctrine of the incarnation and continues, even if disputed, to this day. Christianity is distinguished not only by claims about Jesus Christ but also by the worship that accompanies them.

Pastors handle people's beliefs, teach religious practice and, for many, embody the Christian tradition and so make it available to them. They, therefore, particularly need a means of holding this experiential aspect to Christian theology at the heart of their activity and thinking. Theologians tend to regard religious experience as less than reliable, and accordingly assign it little evidential value. Pastors are also theologians, but for them, by contrast with their academic colleagues, religious experience is a crucial component in their life and ministry. Their own experience of God sustains them; they cannot claim to be God's servants without being able to give personal content to the term 'God'. Even more, as *Christian* ministers, their interpretations of religious experience are Christian and so embody in the here-and-now of the Church's life in the process by which in history the idea of the incarnation developed. They affirm both the tradition which is described as the Christian faith and the continuing experiences of God which it comprises.

But that is not all. Those who are not believers, for instance, with justification expect the Church and its ministers to stand for the phenomenon of religious experience. This may be ridiculed, dismissed or queried, but that claimed experience is the point at which non-believers identify believers and so may legitimately expect to have some idea of what they are dealing with. And, of course, the converse is true for believers, who search to have their present experiences of God intensified or to acquire new ones. Religious experience is the foundation of the Church's and the pastor's life. It links belief and practice, believer and non-believer, and the welter of confused expectations from inside and outside with which the Church works.

Religious experience, therefore, has to be assigned value as a datum in our theological reflection. But it cannot be isolated from common human experience, the basic component of which is relationships. This theme confronts us when we reflect both on our ordinary human experience and on religious experience, particularly in the context of the classic of the incarnation. Relationships are not ends in themselves. Through them we construct our personal development and social life. We need, therefore, to consider the underlying human dynamic that they involve in order to see how we might today interpret the way that God addresses us in this aspect of our human experience.

Much of our life is lived on the basis of our earliest experiences as we resolve, repeat or re-use them. None of us begins life alone. Even the most deprived person starts life in a relationship, first with a mother but soon with other people. All such relationships are ambiguous. They include good and bad feelings alike, and these have to be dealt with. As a result, relating to another necessarily involves our projecting aspects of ourselves on to them. If we like these, we may as a result seek closer attachment to that person. If, however, we dislike those parts of ourselves, we may try to punish or dismiss them there [Klein 1959]. This basic quality of human life accounts for much of the bewilderment that we so often feel in our own relationships or those which we observe between others.

At the level of our unconscious behaviour every relationship is more turbulent than we may realize. Destructive rage, for example, may dominate. This is a characteristic of our earliest experience, with which we live all our lives and with which we usually learn to cope. We are not simply driven to strong feelings of anger or anxiety by things outside us. That world interacts with our inner world of the developing self and profound unconscious attitudes are generated.

Small children provide the best examples of this, since they tend to express their feelings freely. These are often more violent or full of rage than anxious parents find comfortable or understandable. The baby seems to be living in a turbulent world from the first, even though to a large degree protected by its mother from outside pressures. The experience is one of conflict — 'either/or' rather than 'both/and'.[1] As we mature, however, our world and our connection to it take on different patterns as we shift from 'or' to 'and' and the new problems and opportunities this offers. We generally move from rivalry to a more secure sense of identity as what had seemed threateningly destructive begins to be seen as something whole to which we can relate. From that relationship hope emerges. This process is most prominent in two periods in our lives: first, when as a baby we begin to perceive our mother as a distinct person other than ourselves, and as someone to whom we relate rather than one on whom we depend; and second, when in a sense we repeat the procedure as part of growing up into adulthood. It is always amazing how the teenager's ogre father can be transformed by a few years into a friend and colleague.

A similar process can also be discerned in a group when a pairing dynamic prevails. Two members are loaded with feelings in the hope that they will produce what is needed. This allows other members to evade responsibility for the powerful, and often painful or even destructive, feelings which they themselves need to acknowledge and make use of if anything is to be achieved. An atmosphere of expectancy is created. For example, there are churches where a shifting pattern of small groups is the usual mode of life. Here hopefulness for the inner life of the church is sustained: something is always *going to* happen — new life, new vision, new mission. Meanwhile, a rationale as to why things do not happen is created by projecting outside the group and there locating the hindrances — the demands of living, pressure of work, financial problems in young families, and the like. The process develops its own intensity. The linking may become more specific and produce the notion of an idealized leader who is created in the mind and longed for: this person, it is believed, will bring needed resources and charisma. When such fantasies are focused in an individual, any drawbacks are ignored. Outsiders are often mystified that blatant weaknesses or unsuitability are overlooked. But the groups within that church continue, at least for a while, to create this desirable fantasy, largely so that they will not have to relate seriously to each other.

Two fundamental qualities of common human experience emerge from this discussion, both of which need to be addressed in any contemporary thinking on the incarnation. First, as individuals we grow as we acknowledge and work with the sense of *limitation* which mature people have to recognize in themselves. From almost our earliest infancy we have to come to terms with the fact that there is both what is 'I' and what is 'Not-I'. This may seem obvious, but to acknowledge that there is something other than us implies restriction. Yet every human being needs to come to terms with this limitation, the bounds to himself and his existence which in fact enable him to develop at all.

Second, people exist as persons only when they *negotiate* with one another. There is no self-sufficient individual life. Throughout our lives we live by accepting the limitations to ourselves and to others. These make it possible in practice for us to have anything to do with each other and so to enter into relationships. Through these relationships hope is generated, one of the primary characteristics of what it means to be human.

Human relationships, therefore, can never be simple. To speak casually of 'relate' and its associated ideas, as preachers and pastors are inclined to do, may obliterate this range of inevitable complications and so give people a false sense of themselves, of their neighbour, and, therefore, ultimately also of God.

Limitation and Negotiation

Relationships are full of excitement and feelings of one sort or another. By contrast 'limitation' and 'negotiation' sound cold and formal. But these two words refer to fundamental aspects of human life which both the pastor, who tries to embody the model of the incarnation, and the theologian, who offers ways of interpreting it, need to explore in order to speak in our present age.

Limitation is essential for growth. As we develop, we

progressively become aware of ourselves ('I') by distinguishing this from what is other ('Not-I'). But the individual does not do this in isolation. Even ignoring the period of gestation, we can see that our earliest moments of life are lived in the unit of mother-child. We are not self-sufficient. So the growth of the self is a continuing process of discovering what is both I and Not-I. We begin to recognize limitations to our selves or, as we might call them, 'boundaries'. We then use them as the means by which we assert our individuality. For example, when we are newly born our first perceptions are probably of near-fusion with our mother's breast. Mother and child are closely knit and the boundaries around two individuals are blurred. Growth, however, depends upon our progressively distinguishing our self from that breast, getting the boundaries clearer, until we (both child and mother) generate a relationship.

As we become more aware of ourselves we discover the second vital feature of life together. Once disabused of a sense of fusion, we have to devise ways of staying in touch with others. The outcome is our second chief characteristic — negotiation. This is founded on mature recognition of others. We learn that life is made up of relationships that we negotiate with others. We discover how we are related to complex, dimly felt but important, networks of human institutions, like families. So, for example, a child first negotiates with its mother through demand and response. The early words of 'I want' lead to the familiar ploys of child and mother, and the struggles begin. But the child's world is not confined to its mother. There are other people, such as a father, relatives and friends, not to mention animals. The physical world impinges. And running through all these there is the substructure of connections and associations in which the adults who inhabit the child's world are caught up. At an early stage, for example, a child may experience his mother's behaviour as irrational and incomprehensible. Her responses to the child may not feel congruent with his demand or he may not be able to make sense of her attitude towards him in terms of his own perception of the world at that moment. But this confusing experience also makes him aware of that wider world of feelings and influences, which is greater than his immediate environment, to which he contributes and with which he will have to deal throughout his life.

Limitation and negotiation are also crucial in religious experience. The categories of 'I-Thou' and 'I-It' [Buber 1937] are usually taken as clarifying those distinctions between persons and things, or between the personal and the impersonal worlds, which are necessary for religious experience. But a more important issue is the assumption behind them that difference, and hence the need to manage limitation, is essential for life. Intense religious experience, such as that of the mystic, might seem to have little to do with limitation. It implies a loss of the self in oneness with God. But even this experience is only possible in so far as God and man remain distinguishable. The most profound mystical moments, when the mystic claims fusion with God, preserve this distinction by being temporary. There is no permanent mystical state. The intense quality of such experiences, which momentarily blur human individuality, is compensated for by their short duration [Katz 1978]. It is not the experience itself which cannot be tolerated; it is the loss of boundaries, or failure of our needed limitation, which implies death.

For most people, however, religious experience is less intense and more provisional than this. The half-believer, with a wistful longing for the full-blooded belief of which he or she feels incapable and an inability to abandon belief which will not let him go—permanently oppressed by a 'forgotten dream'—is prominent in religion, especially today [Baelz 1975]. Ministers spend much time with such people, and this experience seems at least as common (and is probably even more so) as that of the religiously intense. Hovering between belief and unbelief, the Christian half-believer is sustained by a twofold awareness: a sense of some sort of God, albeit vague and indeterminate, and a recognition that the way of Jesus is important and admirable. By this twofold stance the half-believer identifies himself: there is limitation, by virtue of his capacity to believe in comparison with the wish to believe; and negotiation, since the relationship between the half-believer and his longed-for God and admired Jesus has constantly to be negotiated in the light of this limited capacity to believe. The two basic themes of human life, therefore, re-emerge in a familiar religious experience.

Religious experience, therefore, whether intense or fragile, points to limitation and negotiation. Both demand that some disjunction between the believer and God is preserved, as is confirmed by the classic of the incarnation. The half-believer's experience, however, further demonstrates an important point for this doctrine. For it is given an explicitly Christian orientation by preserving a distinction between God and Jesus. However intimate the connection may be, a distinction (or, we might say, a limitation, so that negotiation can occur) is essential if the religious experience of the half-believer is to be possible. So this experiential indicator directs us to the classic core of incarnational theology, but bases it on a form of religious experience which is a specific instance of common human experience.

Whether we begin with the common human experience of infancy and growth, or start with specifically religious experience, the outcome is the same. By either route we reach the complementary ideas of limitation and negotiation. Our experience of limitation is that it enables us to be sufficiently aware of our own selves that we can approach and be approached by others. This process is about drawing boundaries so that we can identify ourselves and be identified by others — the basis of all relationships.

The complementary notion is that of negotiation. Individuals and groups use boundaries, as they become aware of them, as points for negotiation with others and with the world, and so they create new things. This newness may be personal — our growth — or it may belong to us and to others as together people come to a renewed perspective on some aspect of our world. But such developments come about only as we discern our boundaries, whether as individuals, groups or even societies, and so can confidently negotiate with others.

This way of seeing human life and behaviour is emerging in the present century as people explore what it means to be human. The question for the pastor as theologian, however, is critical: Given this range of human behaviour, much of it drawing the minister's attention to the unconscious dimensions of life, how can we today conceive of and speak about God encountering us? If we cannot address this question, then we have found part of human life from which, wittingly or not, the claims of God have been excluded. Such a conclusion, however, is inconceivable for the believer. What ideas about the incarnation, therefore, may emerge when we give specific attention to these understandings of our human life and of the pastor's involvement with it? This question may involve neglecting some other no less useful themes. For the pastor, however, such selection is essential. We have to discover what happens to the Christian classic of the incarnation when we base our thinking upon the data which the pastor continually encounters via common human experience and specific religious experience alike.

Incarnation, Limitation and Negotiation

When we use the categories of limitation and negotiation, we are freed from the constraints which usually dominate discussion about the incarnation. Traditionally these have concerned identity. But by emphasizing differences (limitation) and how they are employed (negotiation), we may find a contemporary way of holding together and illuminating our faith in the incarnation and our pastoral practice deriving from it.

a) Limitation

Every approach to the incarnation has to grapple with limitation. Kenotic[2] theories may in themselves be inadequate, but their emphasis on self-emptying and surrender (what we could call 'limitation') lies at the heart of all reflection on the incarnation. If we pursue the idea of limitation using common human experience as our reference, we first note that limitation is essential for growth and development. In this light it is neither constricting nor diminishing. It describes the way in which we acquire and consolidate the boundaries by which we define ourselves in relation to others. From this sense of limitation the centre of attention becomes not our (individual) inner life but how we act with others in various settings — our roles. There is no absolute distinction between person and role, but it is one worth making as a help towards clarity in thinking about the significance of limitation for the classic of the incarnation.

Take, for example, a normally growing girl. We are not usually very concerned to diagnose her inner motivations and how they may or may not be expressed. The important point is the way in which, as a child in relation to different contexts—mother, father, social setting and so on—she is being defined and defining who she is. Her inner life is highly relevant, but we do not have to become preoccupied with it and with data from it, to which we have little or no access. In most circumstances we can know enough about her and her development through how she behaves and what she does. This gives us sufficient grounds on which to make judgements and to respond to her.

The same principle applies to our theological reflection on Jesus Christ. We live without information about him, particularly his inner life and motivations. These will always be questionable and be an area in which the faithful projectively explore their faith. This, as we shall see in our examination of the atonement, is not illegitimate behaviour; it is precisely God's intention in making himself vulnerable in this way. Our inevitable ignorance, however, is not worrisome. Jesus' public self, as told in the stories of the Gospels, and the dealings with others that it engendered are sufficient for us to begin to reflect on the significance of God's use of that limitation which is basic to all human experience.

The debate about what may be known of Jesus of Nazareth continues. Underlying it is the long-standing argument over the connection between the man of Nazareth and what believers confess about him, sometimes called the debate between 'the Jesus of history' and 'the Christ of faith'. This distinction, however, although significant in biblical and theological studies, seems to have had little impact on the Church at large. Ministers have tried to use it in teaching their congregations, but there are few signs of its having taken root there. Current liturgical revisions do not recognize it. The concepts of limitation and boundaries, however, suggest why this may be so and take us further into an important area for incarnational thinking. The distinction between the Jesus of history and the Christ of faith is not something outside of us which we can debate. Thus it is not first about Jesus, but it directs attention to the negotiation which we each continually make between who we are (our inner selves) and what we are (ourselves as seen and used by others). We can describe this more tersely as the continuing negotiations between our person (who we are) and our various roles (what we are).

The word 'role' carries unfortunate overtones of acting or playing. It may suggest a mask which can be taken up or laid down at will. In religious contexts this may imply hypocrisy: if I am playing a role, I am not myself acting with integrity. But the term is used here more precisely, not of something assumed or laid down but of a function which is performed in relation to a task. This, as it stands, is a little cryptic. It needs explaining, and the best way to do that is through an illustration.

The role of father is a function of a family; that of priest is a function of the Church. Without 'family' — mother and child — 'father' has little or no meaning; similarly, without 'Church', however we interpret that large term, we cannot understand 'priest'. But no role is simple. Because it is a function it will be affected by what an organization — say, a family or a church — is doing. In addition, we all simultaneously occupy several roles in life, which leads to conflict between them. The key point, however, is that, whatever the role, it *always* has to be negotiated. My inner motivation, why I have elected, say, to be a parent or a priest, can be explored, but it remains a concern which I may or not care to share. As roles, however, 'father' or 'priest' are different. They are not private to me but are created through negotiation with others as they make their assumptions about me and explore what I may represent for them. I may have a view of my role as parent, but I do not determine it; it can only be thought of in relation to others, first the immediate family and then the wider range of a cultural setting and its assumptions about parenthood. The same is true of 'priest' and of any other role. Because it is negotiated with others, its chief mark is that it is available for public scrutiny as against the privacy of the person.

Such scrutiny, however, cannot be done from a distance. It brings people together and invites them to test the points at which their lives, beliefs and fantasies impinge on one another. The term which we have already used, 'boundary', now comes into play to describe these points of scrutiny. When two people, groups or organizations do anything together, they work with a series of perceptions of themselves and each other. A church, for example, may think of itself as the embodiment of God's love in a place; those to whom it turns, however, may see it as the place in which to locate their fear of death and the unknown. This does not mean that there is no way for the two groups to meet. But the church's sense of its boundary, what it thinks it stands for to other people, and other people's sense of their boundary in relation to that church, need to be appreciated. This way of drawing boundaries follows when we recognize limitation as one way by which we define ourselves and are defined by others. A church, for instance, cannot be just what it likes to think it is; it is limited to some extent to what it is also allowed to be by others. We all experience this. Today it is frequently called a communication problem. The concept of a boundary, however, can help us focus on the issue as it is, rather than leap too quickly into explanation. It helps to discern the interface between what I think I am and what other people make me or wish me to be, where my person and roles coincide.

Pastors regularly work in this area as they and those with whom they minister negotiate the distance between their self-image as a Christian minister and people's assumptions about them as, say, a holy person or God-man. Neither our own definition from within nor the view of others alone constitutes the role: it is created and becomes useful through that negotiation which becomes possible when the importance of limitation (boundaries) is recognized. Without this, we might say, there is no pastor, but only one person's fantasies about himself and a set of images held by others. Boundaries are therefore a means to personal development and to collaborative endeavour. They are creative and limitation is, paradoxically, not limiting.

This theme is important for thinking on the incarnation, as we shall discover below. We should note, however, that, although the term 'limitation' (and its variants) has a long history in reflection on the incarnation, I am proposing it here and discussing it within a specific context. It directs us to accessible material and the idea of role rather than any preoccupation with questions of inner drives or motivation. For the moment three points need to be held in mind.

First, 'limitation' (and the associated idea of 'boundary') draws attention to the important fact that difference and separation are the only means that human beings possess for establishing relationships. The idea of knowing someone is more complex and profound than is sometimes realized. Limitation as a concept offers us a way of sustaining the idea of relationship at the centre of our thinking without slipping into fantasies about what we know of ourselves and of others.

Second, the notion makes use of the distinction between person and role, thus emphasizing the way that people become available to one another and consequently vulnerable to mutual scrutiny. Whatever we may be in ourselves ('I' or 'Jesus of Nazareth'), this is not separable from whatever we are in relation to others ('my roles' or 'the Christ of faith'). Thus two traditional themes of the doctrine of the incarnation —God's accessibility and vulnerability—emerge once again (but from a new perspective) as foundational for the classic. They are not the results of some divine choice but are necessary conditions of any relationship within the classic, whether between God and man, or Jesus and God, or man and man, or Jesus and his developing self.

Third, questions of the unconscious world, which we have already shown to be so significant for the contemporary world and consequently for theology, are not confined to a fruitless attempt to explore and even analyse Jesus' psychological make-up. They are involved in interrelation, as seen in the many pairs of the classic, and in the notion of role, by which people (including Jesus Christ) become available for scrutiny.

b) Negotiation

Negotiation is more briefly described. Since the kernel of the doctrine of the incarnation is a series of pairs, Jesus Christ cannot be considered except in terms of them. A relationship between him and God is basic. It is presumed, for example, by the stories of Jesus at prayer, in particular the cries from the cross. He is also defined through significant interchanges with other people. The relationship between Jesus and his neighbour, whoever that is at any moment, is a central theme in the Gospels, and was rapidly picked up by the early Church. These two negotiations—with God and the neighbour—have also proved crucial in the believer's experience down the ages, and they remain so. Christians claim that Jesus is an access point to God. His dealings with God, therefore, are obviously vital. But negotiation between Jesus and his neighbour is also essential, because the believer himself is one such neighbour. For us to have access to God through Jesus Christ we need both these links—Jesus and God, Jesus and neighbour.

There is, however, a third, but more complicated, link in our human lives which must also find a place in any doctrine of the incarnation—that between the self and the developing self. As we grow we renegotiate within ourselves what we were and what we are becoming. The loss of innocence is one example of this. Something happens to us and, as a result, we have to negotiate a shift from what we formerly were, innocent and ignorant, to what we now are, knowledgeable but different, even corrupted. If we do not manage such transitions, we can get stuck either in the process itself or in a fantasized former state, pretending that nothing has happened. Every transition involves negotiation. We abandon one state or attitude as we take up a new one. Usually this happens without our realizing it. But on reflection we may discover what took place and find ourselves unexpectedly wistful. Any gain is accompanied by a sense of irreplaceable loss.

This aspect of our ordinary experience invites us to reflect upon Jesus' self-consciousness in a new way. We have already noted that we can never know specific details about this. But neither can we discount the development in his life that is presented in the Gospel writers' accounts and in the early theological reflections upon these. Each Gospel from its own perspective presents a Jesus who in his adult behaviour shows signs of growth like any human person. St Mark, for example, describes the beginnings of his ministry as tentative. Jesus indiscriminately heals people and then retires to pray. Against the disciples' pressure he refuses to return, but moves on with a more clearly stated task: 'I have to proclaim my message . . . That is what I came . . . to do' (Mark 1.38). The next healing indicates this change. It is specifically set in the social and religious context of the day: Jesus sends the cured leper to conform to the law's requirements. But in this new law-confirming stance we can foresee the conflict with the authorities which will finally crucify him.

This type of shift from first enthusiastic encounters to maturer ministry is not peculiar to Jesus. It is an instance of that common human experience of having to struggle at every moment with who we are and the transition into what we are becoming. This is, notoriously, the distinctive problem of adolescence; nevertheless it affects us throughout our lives. Although, therefore, Jesus' negotiation between his self and developing self must remain hidden, the idea that he, like us, was caught up in it is necessary. While the details of such development are unknowable, it does not follow that the fact cannot be acknowledged.

The themes of limitation and negotiation are integral to any contemporary reflection on the incarnation. They are also ways of approaching the question of transference, a key mode by which we relate to one another. Although a technical concept in psychoanalysis, this process of human interaction, it will be recalled, is not confined to that setting. During analysis the boundaries within which transference is going to be risked are carefully defined because of the powerful material that is likely to be unlocked. They are also drawn in everyday life, although by no means so precisely. Sometimes such boundaries are sanctioned by convention. For example, confidentiality is generally ascribed to the religious role of the priest in the confessional. This enables the priest/penitent relationship to be used transferentially for that between God and the penitent.

Since, however, such transference is a facet of common human experience, especially when a pair is concerned, the crucial question for the pastor as theologian is how God engages with us at this unconscious level of our being. That, theologically, is where the classic of the incarnation comes in. The two themes of this classic are pairs — God *and* Christ; God *and* mankind; Christ *and* me — and differences. We have noted how fundamental pairings are to all human life and experience. Today we need to bring the concepts of limitation and negotiation, and the particular way that they come together in the idea of transference, to bear on the way that we might think of the incarnation, in the context of our pastoral practice and Christian discipleship.

c) Incarnation

Life is composed of a series of relationships which can neither be segmented into unconnected pairs nor blurred into an undifferentiated whole. Transference demonstrates that we regularly shift perspectives between different relationships as a way of bringing about change. The result is some new possibility and way of living—that is, hope. Thus someone, a person who is not my father, can be sufficiently 'father' for me to deal with some unresolved issue in my life involving myself and my relationship with others. This does not necessarily come about through formal treatment; it is a facet, usually unrecognized, of everyday living.

The classic of the incarnation is precisely about this question, inviting us to see how various relationships can be opened up, given new dimensions and explored through one another. For instance, it invites us to enlarge our perspective on the perennial social problem of how I live with my neighbour by transferentially using my relationship with God. In this, through some religious activity—worship or prayer— God can become 'neighbour' and thus invite us to deal with an aspect of ourselves which may need opening up and profound change. Or, as is more familiar to Christians, if I wish to become clearer about my relationship with God and his with me, I am invited to do this by first exploring what is occurring in my relationship with my neighbour. These are examples of the way that transference permeates the Christian tradition.

The criterion which applies to transference, whether in a specific or generalized sense, is 'usability'. This is not the same as usefulness, but describes the capacity of someone or something to be employed by others as a means of testing the value of something. It refers to how accessible a relationship can become to those involved so that it can be used for more than its own immediate and obvious ends. For example, a vicar may be approached for counsel. But in addition to what he says, an important factor in the meeting is his 'usability'— that is, his willingness to accept that he may also (and even more importantly) be being used by the person who comes to assign importance to the problem itself. He or she is thus immediately assured that what is concerning them is important. There is nothing that the minister can do about this; it is a function of his usability alongside whatever usefulness he may provide in the actual counselling.

Here we reach the heart of the classic of the incarnation. The theme of God becoming one with us is less important than his action in being deliberately caught up in our world of transference, where the criterion is not association (being with) but availability (being used). For God to be with us (Emmanuel) becomes not just identification with us. It is more profound: God's chosen criterion by which he is to be judged is the extent of his availability to be used by his divine creation. This is because transference is using one relationship (usually an intimate and intense one) in such a way as to allow new experience of another.

But how might God offer such usability? And what is the significance of the classic of the incarnation for it? In our everyday experience of transference, talk, although important, is never enough. Although the experience of transference is one of feeling, this is often too deep to be articulated or too vague to be spoken clearly. These feelings cry out for interpretation. And this, too, gives us a clue about the incarnation. For the process of interpretation is one of joining in usability. The interpreter, when caught up in transference, does not provide the answer or the solution to someone's problem. He is at the time part of the problem. Together, however, the pair can seek to clarify what the transference is about, to expose at least some of the connection implicit in it, and then invite action in response.

In our dealings with God verbal interpretations of our lives are not even available. People who stress the present word of God in Scripture do not on the whole argue that it is specifically directed to individual moments. Such use has a taint of magic. With him interpretation is therefore, as in everyday experience, always more than words. God's interpretative stance, as we join him in the various transferences by which we live, lies in the model of activity which he offers in the incarnation of Jesus Christ. This is why Jesus Christ can be called 'the word of God', or, as a result of our present discussion, 'God's interpretation'. This Jesus, like any other person, is not solely identified from within but comes to be as boundaries are negotiated. This also makes him, like any other person, vulnerable. But in our everyday world of transference he becomes usable, that is, he becomes God.

The gospel, therefore, does not offer understanding—that is, certain knowledge of human life, its hopes and fears, its dilemmas and ambiguities. Although it is at times proclaimed as if it did, this is to pretend to have dealt with, and so, by implication, to have dispensed with, something basic to our lives. The result is a dehumanizing of people and a devaluing of their lives and experience to which religion is occasionally prone. The gospel of God incarnate offers an inexhaustible model for interpreting the basic experiences of every human life, which is lived in relationship and therefore is dominated by transference.

In this light the incarnation is not a doctrine about God's being one with us; nor does it feed our aspirations to become one with God. Incarnation is God's statement of his willingness to be used in the confused human dynamics of transference. The two primary components of our human development, limitation and negotiation, appear as aspects of God's life too. In Jesus, however, we see them transformed as the priority that we tend to assign to personal growth is consciously subordinated to activity in role. Jesus, like any of us, displays the self-orientated aspects of our common human experience but consistently deploys them on behalf of others— God and his neighbour. For example, each Gospel portrays him becoming aware, as he moves towards the Passion, that, while he remains responsible for his own actions, he is undertaking them on God's behalf. The struggle in Gethsemane is a specific instance, but the same theme appears in the presentations of Jesus' death: the paradox of holding control of events by surrendering it [Vanstone 1982]. Acting fully on his own authority but exercising it on behalf of others is the theme throughout his ministry. This brings him into conflict with some and makes him a source of wonder to others. The fragility of any pair—in this case those between Jesus and God and Jesus and his neighbour—is not denied. On the contrary, our attention is consistently drawn to it and it is acted upon, until ultimately it is confirmed in the cry of dereliction from the cross.

When we reflect on the incarnation we are considering material that is not easily accessible. This sometimes leads to theorizing which does not impinge on ordinary life and which the pastor accordingly rejects or ignores. But underlying both the stance suggested here and the minister's experience is the obvious point that the only evidence available to us about people's inner lives or of what is going on in any relationship is public behaviour. Hypotheses about people can be based only on what we can scrutinize. In the case of the incarnation the evidence for the pairings that we have discerned lies both in the handed-on stories about Jesus and in the commitment of believers to faith in him.

These pairings can be examined in the light of the critical test of relationships that we have just noted: how differences are made to work and, more importantly, for whom. In other words the criterion is how available a relationship is for use transferentially by others.

First, there is the relation between God and Christ, as displayed in Jesus' teaching and ministry. This proves secure enough to resist pressure to separate his activity from that of God. Jesus did not contest God's responsibility for his world nor did he shirk his own responsibility. He can, therefore, be available for use as a focus for our transferences concerning God. It is perhaps because of this strong sense of his own responsibility and therefore authority that he gives short shrift to hypocrites, those who publicly aspire to responsibility without taking it, so displacing it on to others.

Second, when we consider Jesus in relation to his neighbour, whoever this is at any moment, we find as a mark of his ministry that no person has to be diminished in order to encounter Jesus, and through him God. They are able to become something for one another, and so the differences between them may become usable. Thus the simple and the wise, the strong and the weak alike are recognized and affirmed for what they are, being offered new chances, but are not abused by being 'understood'. Instead they are caught up in the necessarily joint activity of interpretation.

Third, the external pressure upon the inner life of Jesus,

between his person and the several roles which he occupies and with which he struggles, seems not to have exposed any weakness. His relationship with himself continues integrated and provides that assurance of reliability (responding to our inevitable dependence) which is a precondition of work at issues of transference. Thus to whichever pairing we turn, each remains intact enough for people, both then and now, to use it as a model which they can embody in themselves and their own life and as a reference by which to interpret this life in various relationships.

This is why the incarnation remains a central Christian classic. The various theological arguments have their days. But functionally they represent the intellectual effort necessary to sustain a working model. Ministers inevitably find practical questions paramount. They are, however, no less concerned with questions of truth. But theirs is the additional nagging question: Why does the incarnation matter for these people, believers and unbelievers, with whom I live and work?

The temptation is to isolate on the one hand the theological problems of the incarnation, while on the other hand trying to sustain a Christian proclamation of God with us and the Church's worship of this Christ. Succumbing to this, however, the pastor, and eventually the Christian Church, will split what, as we have seen, is crucially held together in the classic of the incarnation. For where there are pairs, division is always likely to occur. 'And' is in danger of becoming 'or'. We have noted that pairs in this classic go beyond those on which theologians customarily focus. They are not only about the relation between Godhead and manhood in Jesus Christ, but as they are used they extend to every area of human life through the underlying issue of relationship. The focus thus becomes less on the person of Jesus Christ, significant as that is, than on the model of divine activity which is offered for us, which may be summed up as 'the criterion of usability'.

Yet this does not make theological criteria merely pragmatic. The incarnation turns out to be what historically it has been confessed to be—God's ultimate invitation to his creatures to explore him, ourselves and our neighbours. Limitation, negotiation and transference are confirmed as God's way of enhancing his usability for all mankind. When we see this, the remarkable presentation of Jesus in the Fourth Gospel is illuminated:

> [I pray] that they may be one. As you, Father, are in me and I in you, may they also be in us, so that the world may believe that you sent me. I have given them the glory that you have given me, so that they may be one as we are one: I in them and you in me, that they may be made perfectly one; that the world may know that you sent me and loved them, as you loved me. (John 17.21 – 23)

This meditation on the incarnation, put in the mouth of the incarnate one himself, directs us precisely to the series of pairs that we have discerned. But before examining the significance of these for our pastoral ministry, we must briefly consider the other facet of pairs — production. Every relationship discloses itself in what it produces. (This frequently causes embarrassment, as, for example, when parents have to see themselves in unacceptable aspects of their children. Traditional sayings like 'He's a chip off the old block' or gospel proverbs like 'You shall know them by their fruits' have been confirmed and to some extent expounded by contemporary behavioural study.) The pairings in the incarnation are no exception.

Incarnation and the Kingdom of God

Either the Christian Church or the Holy Spirit might be thought of as outcomes of the pair of God and Jesus Christ in the incarnation. The Church may not be an extension of the incarnation, but it exists and lives by the model of the incarnation. The Holy Spirit, according to the Western creed, 'proceeds from the Father and the Son'. However, the idea that best sums up the outcome of the incarnation, and which we may note in passing, also takes into reckoning both Church and Spirit: the Kingdom of God.

The Kingdom is not identical with the Church. That implicit triumphalism has been done away with, not least in the humiliating experience of the Church during the twentieth century. But a connection between the life and work of the Church and God's activity, which we call 'the Kingdom of

God', is indisputable. Similarly with the Spirit. A major recovery in recent times has been the demanding future dimension of the Spirit. He disrupts any individual or church which claims present completeness. But this experience of the Spirit firmly links it with that orientation towards the future which is found in the concept of the Kingdom of God.

The idea of 'the Kingdom of God' is contested, but some consistent themes emerge. It cannot be located, but represents the movement of God's activity in which he invites men and women to share. The Kingdom is better regarded as opportunity than as event or happening. To be 'not far from the kingdom' (Mark 12.34) is to begin to participate with God, even if unwittingly, and so become an occasion for unexpected divine working. But God's opportunity does not begin with Jesus and his proclamation of the Kingdom. Jesus affirms what had hitherto been perceived as God's ways of acting by demonstrating a new style to it. The chief difference lies in the way in which God's work now becomes more open to human scrutiny.

But the revelation focused through Jesus invites us to look anew at God and ourselves. When we are sensitive to God in his creation we employ our conscious selves through reflection and intellectual apprehension and exploration, or through our aesthetic response to music, art or literature. These familiar aspects of religious life, however, also involve our unconscious selves, although necessarily we are generally unaware of this. Yet now that we have been alerted to our unconscious world and its significance, as well as to the ways in which conscious and unconscious behaviour mesh, the question is not whether God engages with our unconscious, but, How can we think about his encounter with that aspect of ourselves?

The classic of the incarnation, through its emphasis on pairs and their usability, affirms that God is involved with our most fundamental human aspects. God's new quality of availability in the incarnation lies in the way in which he now offers for scrutiny a specific and intimate pair, God and Christ. There he invites us, using the normal transference which marks our human life, to test and discover for ourselves the two great human issues of relationship—that which we have with God and that which we share with our neighbour. These have always been part of man's religious quest and remain foundational. The distinctively Christian contribution is that God enables these two basic relationships to be explored through his use of a third—the integrating connection that God makes with himself. How this is kept alive and present to believers and through them to others is exactly the theme of the Kingdom. The model of divine activity in the incarnation cannot be left in the past history of Jesus. Teaching, preaching and pastoral practice which do this fall under the judgement of God's continuing activity. People no longer live between present and past alone. The Christian gospel of the incarnation and the Kingdom explicitly adds the dimension of the future.

This idea, which is a commonplace of thinking about the Kingdom of God, affects the way in which the basic issue of transference is understood. Both in the structured analytic context and informally throughout human life, transferences are usually explored between past and present, what we have been and now are [Schafer 1978]. But the model of the incarnation, as this is taken up and continued in the Kingdom of God, shifts the scale to one between present and future. Our life is interpreted primarily in relation to what we are, the roles we at present occupy and struggle to fulfil, and what is necessarily unknown, but impinges on our present life—the future. This gospel is founded upon the premise that no one has to be other than they *now* are in order to come to be someone new.

There is inevitably ambiguity when we think about present and future together. But this brings us back to the question of relationship and salvation with which we began this chapter. This ambiguous sense is a mark of salvation: it is an immediate experience of the here-and-now and includes the uncertainty that arises from its having a future aspect. When two people or groups pair, what is happening in the present is always significant in itself. But every such relationship also bears hope and so carries implications for the future. But the trouble with hope is that the moment it is realized it ceases to be hope. When this happens a relationship may come under unbearable stress, since we sustain our relationships to some extent by this unrealized, and often unrealizable, hope. Marital breakdown, for instance, can often be attributed to the way that the partners did not work between their present, the coming together and investment in each other, and the future, the hope which they were generating and its connection with reality. When such fantasized hope dominates, present activity becomes unrealistic. And this experience is not the prerogative of intimate relations. In religion, for example, this is the point at which religion declines from illusion into delusion.

The salvation which the incarnation offers is new experiences and perceptions of ourselves and God, and consequently of our neighbour and the world. This comes about as we use the opportunities for interpretation that God provides in the various pairings with which we are confronted. We are invited to discover new perspectives on every relationship, however secure and familiar or novel and fragile, by using other relationships which God offers us, most notably his own exposed relationship with Christ.

This process is also suffused with hope. It involves our religious longings, which we express as a wistful desire for continuity [Rycroft 1968]. The relationship with God in Christ saves because God invests not in that relationship itself but in the dynamic of pairing which underlies human existence and in the first place generates all relationships. The incarnation is God's public testimony to this. It is not just a series of complex interrelations within the Godhead and between God and humankind. It is God's vulnerable investment of himself in one of the bases of human life as he has created it—the pair.

Salvation, therefore, cannot be described simply as a relationship. It affects our lives more deeply than that. The pastor's concern with salvation brings together two crucial factors: firstly, the series of relationships which are held within the classic of the incarnation and which issue in the Kingdom of God; *together with*, secondly, the fact that in that incarnation God endorses all these essential human dynamics. Sometimes by comparison with other work—counselling or psychoanalysis—the pastor's involvement with people seems to be shallow. It is not; it is different. Pastoring brings together something profound about humankind and aspects of the essence of God himself.

Before turning to the practicalities of this ministry, we can illustrate this profundity from the gospel stories of Jesus.

There he transforms close relationships between himself and
another into an opportunity for them to explore their
relationship with the origin of their life and their future — God.
This is an instance of transference invited and interpreted.
They can review their place within a world which is larger
than they can know but is none the less felt. The lawyer who
is told the parable of the Good Samaritan, for example, is put
in touch with this larger world but in such a way that he does
not lose his own identity or sense of personal responsibility.
Nor does Jesus reject the roles that are thrust upon
him — teacher, healer or Messiah. He is willing to be usable so
that he can make these attributed roles usable by others.
Peter, for instance, in the confession at Caesarea Philippi
received one such powerful response to his presuppositions
about himself and Jesus and about God and the Messiah. He
was given a chance to reinterpret his life and future. It is also
notable how, almost without exception, the future consequences of these encounters are acknowledged. This tendency,
which runs through Jesus' ministry, becomes the norm in the
encounters in the Passion story. Jesus engages in ministry
with people between their present and the future; there is
little about pasts, and when they do arise, they are dealt with
in so far as they have created a present from which the
person concerned has to find a new life. When, for example,
Jesus heals lepers he deals with them as here-and-now
sufferers without getting into debate about the origins of
their sickness. In the Fourth Gospel, where these aspects of
Jesus' ministry are expounded in a condensed way, the writer
explicitly tells a story about Jesus dealing peremptorily with
that question. To the disciples' question, 'Did this blind man
or his parents sin?', Jesus replies that neither did. The man is
to be given new life by beginning now: 'He was born blind so
that the works of God might be demonstrated in him.' It was
not God's intention to make this man an example, but as a
result of his being blind this moment is the one to be grasped
for interpretation for the benefit of the man, his parents, the
disciples, the bystanders, and Jesus himself (John 9.1 — 3).

We later find the same process recounted in the life of St
Paul. His relationship to God was initially changed on the
Damascus road by his vision of Jesus. This, however, became
usable by Paul only after Ananias had joined him in

interpreting it. He used the neighbour-to-neighbour relationship, instantly establishing a here-and-now link with Saul, as the way for him to begin to grasp his own new relationship with God through Christ. Ananias greeted him, touching and addressing him in the language of a new relationship—'Brother Saul' (Acts 9.17). Ananias became for Paul a usable embodiment of that Christ with whom he had had his original striking meeting. This is an instance of the everyday transference that we have considered earlier. Later, in Romans, Paul was to expound how man's relation with God is exposed for examination by the relationship between Christ and God. And in Romans 7 he goes on to explore how that most difficult relationship, the one between our self and our developing selves, can be unravelled for salvation through other relationships, notably that between the Christian and Christ.

We can derive a third example of the way in which the nature of the Kingdom of God as the outcome of the pairs in the incarnation is demonstrated from everyday pastoral ministry. A man comes with a problem about his marriage. If the minister avoids being pulled into a detailed examination of the past, he or she can free that person to examine his relationship to his wife, at least a little, through his relationship to the minister. He can work on what seems to be happening between his visitor and his own role of, say, man of God (however that is fantasized) and bearer of hope or ideals or assurance. If he can have some sense of the generalized transference that is being employed, two points follow. Firstly he can use his own transferences, say to his model of God in Christ, to help him clarify what is being asked of him. And, secondly, he can offer interpretation to the other about the several relationships which constitute his marriage. The question in such an encounter is not just what has happened; what might happen and what can be expected to happen are significant ingredients. The minister's perspective and ministry are different from the retrospective stance of the counsellor or analyst, even though insights derived from their approaches to human beings will inform pastoral ministry. Christian ministry, like the Kingdom of God, oscillates between present and future.

Conclusion

We can begin to see, therefore, that the doctrine of the incarnation is firmly located both in common human experience and in the particular experience which pastors themselves acquire through their ministering with people. This setting is significant for any theology which seeks to prosper in the contemporary world. The classic of the incarnation must take account of that vast area of human behaviour which now goes under the general heading of our unconscious life. We have seen that there are ways of thinking about it. Theologians would have to take them further in integrating these experiential issues with the persistent philosophical questions. But for the working pastor the important point is to be able to see that the incarnation of God in Jesus Christ is a specific act through which God engages not just generally with this world but specifically with the unconscious dimension of human life. The clue to this lies in the several pairings, which give us both points to latch on to in our thinking about the ramifications of orthodox doctrine and a way into the contemporary theory of the unconscious life of individuals and of groups.

In their pastoral care ministers of the incarnation use a model of activity which embodies this divine, Kingdom-like affirmation of the present in the context of the future. They hold together the various realities about human beings that continue to be discovered in this century and the point of interpretation offered for all these relations by this distinctive Christian classic. Neither human beings nor their relationships are fixed enough to become simple, secure reference-points. Everything is more fluid than maybe we had realized; but it does not follow that it is chaotic. Nevertheless, behind the credal confession 'and was made man', there now appear more powerful dynamics and complications than have hitherto troubled the theologians. But the pastor daily lives with these. Now, therefore, we must ask what effect such a perspective may have upon pastoral ministry.

The Pastor as Theologian

Notes

1   As Melanie Klein has said:

> Resentment increases the feelings of deprivation which are never missing in any infant's life. While the mother's capacity to feed is a source of admiration, envy of this capacity is a strong stimulus towards destructive impulses. It is inherent in envy that it aims at spoiling and destroying the mother's creativeness, on which at the same time the infant depends; and this dependence reinforces hate and envy. [Klein 1963, 26]

2   'Kenotic' (from the Greek *kenosis*, meaning 'emptying') describes theories of the incarnation which, based on Philippians 2.7, emphasize the self-limitation of the divine attributes of the Son of God.

SIX

Incarnation and Pastoral Care

Christian ministers often offer care to individuals and groups in terms of identifying with them. They are inclined to believe that they should (and can) stand where people stand, deriving this from belief in the incarnation. There, so the argument runs, God demonstrates that he is with us. 'Emmanuel', 'God is with us', is invoked. It follows that the Christian stance with people is also exactly this: to be with them.

But the idea is vague and often produces vacuous, if well-intentioned, behaviour. Asked why he is in a factory, ward or school, or what he is doing on a bereavement visit or at some other moment of pastoral care, the minister replies, 'In order to be with you.' But that is unsatisfactory. Since it provides no reason why he should be there, this stance does not give people a latching-on point to the pastor and his ministry or message. They then find it difficult either to know what form of association is expected or appropriate, or whether to reject him at any level—friend, counsellor, priest, outsider, insider, and so on. This is not a matter of personality or religious truth. They are basically unsure with whom they are dealing.

The Seduction of 'Incarnational Ministry'

Such ministry is often called 'incarnational'. But it is based upon a deficient grasp of that doctrine. God does not become incarnate in Jesus Christ merely to be at one with mankind. The gospel goes further and addresses the more important issue: 'Why does he do this?' It also speaks of God's achievement and effectiveness—salvation. The Christian calling, therefore, is not merely to be, but by being and believing to achieve. Without vigilance we can slide into a cycle of mutually confirming belief and inaction. The argument runs: We are involved in people's lives, because they are there, and we are with them as God in Christ is with us. Feelings, especially the more violent ones, which are basic data in ministry, are minimized. In addition this sometimes leads to an attitude which demeans others by implying that we understand them. And when that so-called understanding is claimed on the grounds that God has undergone a similar experience in Christ and that he therefore also 'understands', then our inadvertent callousness is compounded.

Feelings that are aroused in us by our contact with others are not ends in themselves but a tool that can be used to something further. They are the basis on which we minister. But without interpretation these, like all experiences, are of little value. All feelings are significant, since the pastor works in the field of people's feelings and experiences. But when we realize that people also live at an unconscious level, awareness of the fact and significance of feelings and their need for interpretation becomes even more important. Any pastoral encounter arouses a range of feelings in the minister. They derive from various sources — his own self; the person or group with which he is dealing; the context at large; and, although this is often overlooked, from the fact that minister and people are involved together.

A key instrument in ministry, therefore, is our awareness of these dynamics and our sensitivity to the corresponding feelings that are aroused in us. The technical term for such feelings is 'countertransference'. This term has been developed by analysts but, as with transference, its original sense was more general. Freud noted how universal it was when he remarked: 'Everyone possesses in his own unconscious an instrument with which he can interpret the utterances of the unconscious in other people' [Freud 1913, 314].

If the pastor is to use this facet of his experience, he does not have to ape the analyst. Indeed it is vital that he does not, otherwise he will lose his own distinctive points of reference for ministry — the aspects of the incarnation that have formed the basis of our discussion. If I am to be able to use the range of feelings that are aroused in me as I live and occupy my role as minister with other people, I have to be sufficiently confident of my own identity to be able to face them in myself.

So much is obvious. But this can be taken further. In order

to minister to other people we have to recognize that their experience is unique; that we do not and cannot share their feelings; and that, therefore, the notion of being one with them is misleading. When, therefore, we feel out of sympathy with another person's predicament, this may be less a sign of failure than a clue to reality and, therefore, of a way into some act of genuine ministry. Awareness of such limitation is the foundation of engagement with others and the essence of pastoral skill in ministry. Anything that blurs this distinction, whether personal anxiety or theological presupposition, hinders ministry on the model of the incarnation.

Here pastoral practice and theological reflection on the incarnation reinforce each other. The various pairs in the classic of the incarnation draw our attention to philosophical and theological problems about the nature of God and the person of Jesus Christ. But more importantly they also remind Christians that creative relationships with God and with one another are possible only because of such differences. Religious people expend much effort trying to avoid this. We emphasize unity and oneness, either with God, within God, or with one another. This sounds seductively ideal, not least as a release from fragile human relationships and our anxiety about being cut off from the divine source of our being. Similarly in our pastoral ministry we often feel urged towards being at one with everyone—to identify with the poor, the needy, and the casualties of this world. To suggest otherwise seems blasphemous, even though in practice such claimed identity seems to produce vacuous and impotent responses to people.

We become stuck in a bind: we wish to work effectively with people for God's sake and feel obliged to identify with them; but in so doing we reduce the opportunities for genuinely doing something with them. We assume that we understand them and so inadvertently slip into a patronizing stance. As a result we may isolate ourselves more than we know from those feelings in ourselves that come from others, which are the key to effective pastoral activity. From the best of intentions and because of an inadequate theological foundation we prove incompetent at the very point where we most wish to be effective—the pastoral care of people.

Roles and Pastoral Ministry

Escape from this impasse lies in holding to two essentials: difference and feeling. One way to do this is to become less aware of ourselves as persons and more alert to our roles. The model of ministry that Jesus presents confirms this stance. He acknowledged and managed the difference between his person (who he was) and the various roles he was assigned (what people wished him to be). Negotiating this difference within himself, he dealt confidently with people on the basis of those roles, whatever they were. Whether these were defined in relation to God (Messiah), society (teacher, healer) or individuals (carer, brother, friend), they were all used as points on which to build ministry. Similarly, then, on this model ministers are not to strive to be good people who seek to help their neighbours. That may be a pleasant self-image, but it is not useful. We function with roles both in the institutions that sponsor us, the churches, and in the fantasies that people hold about it and us.

In this sense the public minister is not unlike a Messiah. These were the products of traditional Jewish expectation, and specifically of the fantasies that people held about it. Jesus, so far as we can see, did not reject the title (thus accepting a role assigned to him), but avoided endorsing its application to him, most likely for the reason already suggested — the fragile nature of this particular fantasy world. Like him, ministers need to be aware that they are to some extent products of expectations and so be conscious of the wide range of possible, largely fantastic, roles that may be being assigned to them. The pastor can then stay sufficiently in touch with people at a deep level, both so that they can approach him in a way to which he finds himself able to respond and, like Jesus, so as to avoid locking people in fragile worlds of fantasy. This is not an either/or argument. *Who* we are as persons does matter, but for pastoral ministry in human relationships we need a strong sense of *what* we are, our role. The emphasis, established for Christians by the model of the incarnation, is always first upon role and second upon person, because in our assigned roles lies our vulnerability.

Two familiar stories from the Gospels illustrate the point.

In the parable of the Good Samaritan two characters—a priest and a Levite—have their personal responsibility firmly assigned but then act irresponsibly. The victim makes a demand on them as human beings. This is a continuing point of power in that story, from which no person is exempt. But the critical questions that it poses concern roles: Who is my neighbour? What does it mean in a society to occupy a particular role—that of neighbour to anyone? And, by implication, what does it mean to hold other roles, too, such as priest, Levite or Samaritan? We find a similar emphasis in the account of the agony in Gethsemane. This describes Jesus undergoing personal pain, but the issues raised concern the role of God's servant—what that implies about suffering, and what it means to conform to the requirements of that role in such a way that it does not become an unconstructive constraint on further ministry with people.

The criteria derived from these illustrations of the priority of role also apply in a Christian ministry which is based upon the incarnation and informed by it. It centres on roles and responsibilities: What is it to be a citizen, whether of a nation or of heaven? What is it responsibly to act in particular roles—in the family as father, brother, mother, sister, child, or professionally as manager, producer, salesperson etc.? The pastor is invited to help to set these and similar issues in a context, since, when he is approached for counsel or pastoring, he is first being addressed in his distinctive role. No doubt in his own mind he is holding a series of roles as confused as those in the minds of the people who come to him. But it is in his assigned role as a representative of the Church or of God that people first approach him, and on this they also found their expectations of him. These may be primitive and magical, but at heart they are religious.

People may consciously approach the minister with an apparently rational understanding of who they are and who he is. That is not disputed. But underlying this level of behaviour there are also unconsciously held beliefs and fantasies, which may well not be coherently expressed. Therefore, since anyone working with people now knows that their unconscious mind is as important a factor in their (and his own) life as their conscious behaviour, a way of remaining in touch with this is needed. And because in this encounter roles are of first importance, the source from which the minister derives the criteria to assess his own sense of role (both from within and that assigned by those who approach him) becomes critically important. Furthermore, the minister can see now, from the way that his supreme model of ministry, Jesus Christ incarnate, addresses this dimension of human life, that he cannot and should not minimize or ignore it. He is required to be a religious person, not just a counsellor or befriending human being, and is specifically required to be a Christian minister.

Case Study

This case study illustrates these points. It is taken from the recent parochial experience of a vicar in an urban parish.

Two sisters shared a house, where they had lived for many years. One was apparently the stronger, taking decisions and generally managing affairs. The other was correspondingly weaker, to the extent of occasionally needing psychiatric treatment. From time to time, however, a reversal took place and the stronger sister became physically ill and appeared in need of support. People believed that the other sister would be unable to cope, and dreaded the future. However, on these occasions the 'weaker' sister blossomed, becoming responsible and managing the affairs of both sisters. Their roles were reversed; the strong became weaker, the weak became stronger.

The vicar of the parish in which they lived had no particular dealings with the sisters. They did not attend his church, but like several people in their area chose to worship in a neighbouring, somewhat older, church. The 'stronger' sister took a leading role there; the 'weaker' had little or no contact. They knew, however, of the vicar of the parish where they lived and he knew about them. One day he was invited to visit the sisters because the 'stronger' had hurt herself and was confined to the house. While he was there the woman who suffered occasional mental disturbance, the so-called 'weaker' one, treated the vicar as more than a casual visitor. She responded to him as someone who represented God. So before he left he deliberately said prayers with them and later took a house communion, mainly for the 'stronger' sister, but with the other also participating. There is still contact between the sisters and the vicar. Sometimes, but by no means regularly, they are seen in his church.

There is, however, a further facet to this story. It appears that many people round about, not only in the immediate environs where the sisters live but also in what might loosely be described as the local community (the vagueness of this term does not matter here), are aware of the sisters and their changed roles. They talk about them and ask the vicar what is happening and how the sisters are getting on, even though they have no personal or direct connection with them. The pair are a focus of some interest on the part of others, who expect the vicar to know about and in a sense to be able to speak for the sisters.

There are many points which could be made, but three illuminate our theme. First, the behaviour of two women, one of whom has a history of psychiatric disturbance, is at first sight not very significant, except to them. People like this are common enough, and on the large scale of human suffering they are of no special consequence. Nevertheless in practice many others are concerned about them. This suggests that some connection is desired and maintained between the comparatively unimportant lives of the pair and the way that others live in the neighbourhood and contribute to local life. In fact more detail on this can be discerned when the area is studied. Their house is at the edge of a part of the town which has a reputation for being depressing and having a large proportion of dependent people. The medical and social services, for example, regard it as an area of heavy demand. In the context of the whole town it is an area which is held in this dependent attitude because it is the receptacle for other areas' projections of incompetence. Yet when examined the estate is shown to produce key leaders in the basic levels of local life—uniformed organizations, charities and other voluntary associations and activities. The lives of these two women—strong and weak, and their reversed roles—seem to match something about the way that the estate and the rest of the town interact.

This observation would not matter greatly in itself, until we note that the local community appears to have no means of expressing itself formally. Because it is held as a place for dependent people, it seems unable to respond. The vicar, however, is allowed to do this. He lives in the area, moves around it, engages with people at basic levels of their lives — birth, marriage and death, as well as in the fundamental associations that make up local life. Even though many have little or nothing to do with his brand of religious belief, his work and the presence of the church touch the network of life in the area at several points. He is assigned a strange form of authority, to stand for and to affirm that life on that estate does have significance. It is parallel to the woman's assumption that, although she apparently has no intention of joining him in the church, he has authority as God's representative.

The key question, therefore, concerns the vicar's role and usability. His involvement with these two women and the way he is immersed in the life of other groups on the estate, complement each other in assigning him authority to work. And part of that work is to provide a focus where individual life and community living can be interpreted together. He is working in a larger context of ministry and beliefs about the minister than he may immediately be aware. Certainly if he confined his public religious activity to the worship of the church, his private devotions or his pastoring of the members of the congregation, he would not be able to grasp what was happening to him with individuals and groups in the area. His ministry would, therefore, become increasingly bewildering, until, as frequently happens, he would probably decide to leave.

Second, it is worth noting that the vicar is used also by the sisters to assist them in handling a distinctive dimension of their personal dilemma. They do not need him for therapy or care. Therapy is provided when needed by the psychiatric service, and care in any professional sense is scarcely required. Their relationship dynamically functions to maintain a balance between them, and they are competent at ensuring that their contacts with doctors and others serve their requirements. But one of them, at least, demands that the vicar should explicitly be a religious figure and that he acts in an appropriate manner by praying. If, therefore, he were to ensnare himself in a therapeutic stance alone, he would not be able to engage with the sisters. He might for a time seem to be effective in this one-to-one relationship with them, but this would prove a delusion. They do not need counsel. In addition, his opportunities for working with other groups in the parish would be inhibited. If he becomes too involved with the presenting problems of the sisters, he is less usable in making the interpretative links between their lives and what they represent of the people on the estate as a whole. In order to do anything the vicar has to be first what he is expected to be—a religious figure—and to behave in an appropriate way.

The third point relates to the use made of him in the wider setting of the parish. Through him people believe that they can learn about the sisters. One consequence is that through the notional unit of 'vicar-plus-sisters' they are also able to consider wider issues of their community. It is possible to hear, contrary to every other fantasy, that the estate is not full of dependent depressives, but that its members have not only theoretical authority for their lives but practical ability to do something about it. Exploration of this would take us too far from our present brief. But we may note the way in which both the sisters and others have expectations of the vicar, especially that in their lives he will 'know what is happening' and will 'understand'. He is not just any figure. His religious function is explicit with the sisters, and others implicitly use him in this way. The question for him, therefore, is how to make use on more than one front of the sisters and their particular demands, and of the wider area and its less specific, but no less real, needs. One thing is certain: the outcome of such work will not be clear. But that, too, seems to be the character of incarnationally based activity.

We should avoid extravagant claims for such ministry. And there are many other points that could be explored in the history of these two women which might, in due course, be useful for ministry. But this story as examined here demonstrates the nature and style of a genuinely incarnational ministry. It is not simply about 'getting alongside' or 'being with' these people, but about being *used* on several fronts at once. To remain effective there the pastor has to cope with the switching between the roles in which people perceive him. For that the themes of the incarnation are the themes of ministry: boundaries, limitation and negotiation.

Care about *boundaries* appears as the minister avoids copying the analyst or therapist. He is thrown back repeatedly in this case, whether by the sisters or by other people, on the question of which role is being assigned to him at any moment. It is no use his determining himself as 'priest' or 'minister' or 'Christian'. These are too general. He has to try and discover first which role, however insignificant to him in his self-esteem and self-valuation, is being expected of him. Then he has to test how congruent this is with his public role as Christian minister—and he has to do this quickly on his feet. The idea of boundaries is the key to this stance.

The notion of *limitation* appears in the nature of the ministry offered. He is prepared to be used first rather than to think that he must have some understanding about what is happening before he can intervene. Such ministry is always a problem, since you cannot really know what it involves until you are doing it. But that is precisely the nature of the risk which the model of the incarnation demonstrates.

The minister works consciously in his role, by *negotiating* between himself and the others. Praying with an emotionally disturbed woman is not the most exciting definition of Christian ministry, especially if the act is isolated and considered apart from everything else. Whatever the theological significance of such prayer (see below, pp. 105—108), pastoral effectiveness lies not with the woman so much as with the way it establishes the minister's role in his own unconscious mind, so that others can attach their own fantasies to that and so use him in different ways. Thus, because of this fragment of ministry, a range of people, many far removed from the original instance, are enabled better to take up their special roles in the world. This story indicates the central importance of the minister's role, as this is created by negotiation between him and the sisters. Confusion on this point produces some of the strife in contemporary pastoral ministry.

Conclusion

The clergy are sometimes said to have lost their role. As a sociological description this can be discussed, and in those terms there is some evidence in its favour. But there are still public ministers, and people still come to them. The gospel and churches remain. Interactions continue day by day, many

of them obvious—as when people meet, talk, help one another
—but many of them unconscious. No clear correlation has yet
been established between church attendance and Christian
influence in an area. All these issues demand the pastor's
interpretation.

When loss of role is mentioned, it usually means that
pastors have slipped from a self-awareness of their role and
of people's expectations of it into a person-based ministry.
This inevitably exhausts itself. When such a stance is justified
by a naive appeal to an inadequate doctrine of the incarnation
as identification, confusion is generated both in ministers
and in those who look to them for ministry. Such behaviour is
apparently sanctioned by appeal to Christian orthodoxy of
the incarnation. We can now see, however, both on the
theological grounds outlined above and on the basis of the
practice of ministry, that incarnation is not about identification
but about affirming differences in the series of pairs that it
incorporates, and about making these creative and not
destructive.

Appreciating limitation, therefore, is one way to discovering
identity. This is not as an end in itself but in order that the
person, whether Christ or the minister, can be sufficiently
identified so that others can give some shape in their minds
to what they are approaching. Such a minister will not be
self-identified but will be willing to be fashioned by the
fantasies of others. But this world of fantasy so deeply affects
them in their own unconscious mind and disturbs their
assumptions about themselves and their role that they need
assurance that they should be working with such phenomena.
The negotiations that this ministry entails are themselves the
mark of a creative working relationship, from which all
involved can make discoveries. The consequential negotiation,
which marks a creative working relationship, leads to
discovery for all involved—growth or conversion. It is here,
perhaps, that the enigmatic saying of Jesus that anyone who
wishes to save his life must lose it (Mark 8.35) takes on new
meaning. Purposefully setting the person, with its self-interest
and importance, in second place (but not, of course, losing it
altogether—otherwise there could be no feelings with which
to inform the role), we are more free to uncover and explore
the roles that we are being assigned. In that way we find our

points of contact with others, most notably with God and our neighbour, and so discover new life for all, including ourselves.

To make these newly exposed links effective, however, we have to live with them and try to use them. Here the minister represents a specific and easily identifiable example of that ministry for which, in various ways, all Christian people are responsible. When they confidently take up this type of ministry, they are revitalized as persons or, in traditional Christian language, 'born again' and given new life. This is salvation, and the gospel through which God offers it responds to the most basic parts of ourselves as human beings.

First, it accepts that our anxieties about relationships are well-founded and that they are not merely neurotic symptoms. Relationships of every sort are fragile, involving, as they do, the problems of limitation and negotiation that we have discussed. Second, however, it declares that these dynamics are not restrictions on our lives, since God himself has affirmed them in the person of Jesus Christ as his own way of being. Here grace abounds: no human being has first to change or deny their basic humanity, including its unconscious aspects, in order to encounter God. Third, conversion comes about when these fundamental aspects of ourselves are transformed. Because God through the incarnation addresses us at this unconscious level of our being, our relationships are perceived as possessing increased richness and significance. They cease to be foci for mere hopefulness and ultimately for disappointment. Instead they become genuine bearers of realistic hope. Differences between people, the felt gap between God and mankind, and the divisions inside each of us, are not hindrances to life: all are God's means to it. They need not be destructive, because, when they are made usable by others, they generate new life for them and for us.

Finally, therefore, believers are invited both by God and by their neighbours to accept without being distressed the often strange roles which people assign them. But this gives the believer opportunity to embody the presence of God, thus losing himself and to finding life. Using his feelings he interprets these expectations for the benefit of others and not for himself. The minister in particular may have to accept the frightening role of 'God-person', with its overtones of magic, fear and avoidance, just as Jesus had to accept, but not endorse, the unsuitable role of Messiah in order to be usable as the Son of Man. It may even, therefore, be that the pastor's role should be sustained as qualitatively different from that of the laity, in spite of contemporary pressure to minimize any such distinction. With their fear of difference, limitation and negotiation, church people may too casually leap to conclusions about all Christians being one, without reflecting on what any differences may signify in terms of usability.

The incarnation as God's endorsement of the twin themes of limitation and negotiation provides a consistently demanding model of how even in the most sensitive parts of his ministry the pastor's *role* is the effective agent. Those who remain faithful to the role of minister are crucified. Persons merely die. The difference is critical, if the minister is not to delude himself and others.

SEVEN

Incarnation and the Disciples' Prayer

Each of the classics that we are examining is also grounded in Christian discipleship. This is important for our study, since the pastor moves in the world of ordinary human lives and feelings, using contemporary skills as best he can, but without losing sight of his distinctively Christian vocation. This is founded upon Christian belief and practice—in a word, discipleship. The religious practice to which the classic of the incarnation relates is prayer. The key issue which any religious body must address is ultimately how people contact God. An essential means by which this connection is believed to be made is prayer.

Prayer as a General Phenomenon

We are not first thinking of spiritual achievements in prayer, but of the widespread religious phenomenon of prayer through which people attempt to contact God. On this issue contemporary Christians sometimes find themselves out of tune with common human experience. Prayer is one of the most prevalent human activities, yet in the life of the Church it seems increasingly a problem. Prayer is considered essential by most believers, but many regard it as not very useful for achieving practical effect. On the one hand what would it be to be Christian and not pray? Praying is a minimum qualification for being Christian. Meetings begin with the ritual, whether the prayer is perfunctory or fervently extempore. Yet on the other hand praying seems futile. Some claim that prayer is vital and testably influential, but most believers live with uneasy feelings of irrelevance and ineffectiveness. What, for example, do our persistent prayers for social justice or political change achieve? And what of the many prayers for implied personal benefit or advantage? These are

public. Who knows what is said in private? Prayer as
Christian practice is ambiguous. It is a central aspect of
Christian behaviour which nevertheless pushes us to the
margins of our faith. Ostensibly looking to God in confidence,
we find our reflective selves doubting.

Yet this Christian practice harnesses a major area of
common human experience and the Christian classic of the
incarnation. When this is appreciated, new possibilities begin
to appear. 'O God' or 'Jesus', as exclamations of exasperation,
may not sound much like prayers. Yet in a crude fashion they
are. No rational thought is given to whom they are addressed,
but that is rarely the case with any ejaculation. Somewhere
underlying this casualness may still lie a sense of someone or
something other than the self with whom a needed link is
being made. More refined prayers are consciously said, even
by those who claim no allegiance to any church. David Hay
gives a selection of comments from a range of people. All are
about 'connection with God' (here used as a shorthand for the
various descriptions used by different people). He notes that:
'90 per cent of the reports relating to prayer, or premonitions,
or a presence not labelled "God", came from people who
seldom or never went to church' [Hay 1982, 155].

Refining general sociological surveys of implicit, common
or folk religion, by addressing his questions to claimed
experience rather than to publicly observable activity, Hay
was confronted, as he put it, with a series of puzzles. For
example, why at a time when in much of mainland Europe
and the UK church membership and attendance is statistically
low do religious activities like prayer remain so prevalent?
The answer to that question lies beyond the scope of this
study, but we can consider what the fact of such prayer may
evidence.

Prayer expresses expectation. We resort to it when things
are, or seem to be, beyond control. Caught between events
which feel unmanageable and the need to take decisions, we
articulate as an interim measure our hope that by making a
connection with the Almighty (otherwise disregarded, possibly
not believed in, and certainly given little attention as a realistic
resolver of problems) the issue might be better handled. This
is not an expressed intention to do something; that comes
later. It is an ejaculated expectation that we already know is

unlikely to be realized. No one would be more surprised than the utterer at a *deus ex machina*. Prayer as a religious phenomenon is an instance of hopefulness created by making a connection between the praying person and some notion of God.

Discipleship and Prayer

The Christian disciple at prayer, however, claims to be engaged in more than this, and history provides numerous instances of individuals and, through their liturgies, of churches which have refined this practice. This spiritual activity is not itself distinctive; it is rooted in common human experience. Its focus, however, is different. For the Christian Church, prayer is primarily a means by which Christians become increasingly competent in their roles.

Before going further, however, we should now restrict the range covered by the word 'prayer'. People sometimes wish to turn all normal activities into prayer. But such generalizations are not very helpful. If every activity is prayer, what *precisely* is it to pray? Neither can we transform prayer into action; activity itself then merely replaces prayer. The general term 'spirituality' is frequently used to disguise this confusion. That notion stands for the general style of Christian living and we shall study this later (see below, pp. 155—63). Today in our liturgically preoccupied churches we risk confining the idea of prayer to public liturgy and make it part of shared experience. There is a connection between liturgy and praying, but to transform all prayer into a liturgical act also diminishes it.

Prayer, as understood in common human experience, has a specific form. It is intimate, deliberate, noticeably religious and personally questioning. We are dealing in prayer with a conscious, personal direction towards God which has impact upon our unconscious life. Because it takes place in this area, it can be associated with the concept of 'pre-conscious' activity. This describes contents from the unconscious mind which are in principle accessible to our consciousness, such as knowledge and memories that are not at the time conscious but may be nearly so. Prayer occupies a similar region of our spiritual and everyday lives. We cannot, therefore, make everything into prayer without creating confusion and disabling part of ourselves. The term describes what takes place in that part of our being, where connections are made between the conscious and the unconscious minds, between ourselves and God, and between our person and our roles.

From this perspective there is the question of how the role of being a Christian is developed and on whose behalf we exercise it. These two issues point us to the two major types of prayer. The first comprises meditation and contemplation — How is our joining with God established, and on what basis? Spiritual directors distinguish the two, but they are closely connected. For the sake of distinguishing facets of our prayer life, we might think of meditation as concerned with our partnership with God and contemplation as to do with our own self-awareness. These develop our role as Christians. The second form of prayer is intercession, in which prayer is offered for others. That invites us to check at all times the question why this role is created in the first place.

a) Meditation

Meditation in Christian practice is different from those forms of meditating that are urged, for example, upon harassed businessmen. They are encouraged to create restful space within the maelstrom of stress. That space is itself the focus of the meditation, although an object such as a vase of flowers or a statue may be provided to help. Christian meditation, however, is specifically directed to the life, ministry, death and resurrection of Jesus Christ. This is not merely observed or adored. Meditation requires participation. Meditating on the story of Jesus, we become intensely aware of these boundaries between ourselves and God and between ourselves and our neighbours and within our own selves. As we focus outside ourselves on the person of Jesus Christ, we are pressed to try and get straight this series of relations, both outside and within.

These are exactly the connections which are fundamental in the Christian classic of the incarnation and to any sound practice of pastoral ministry. Prayer as meditation, therefore, is not primarily concerned with who is the subject and who the object in the dialogue between myself and God, but with the process itself.

When we meditate on the incarnate Christ, we may hope to become like him. Such hopes are not wishes. There are as many Jesuses as there are fantasies that we can have about ourselves — gentle and considerate, a powerful teacher, an exorcist, the confronter of tyrants or scourge of religiosity. These may confirm the beliefs that some people hold, but they render the Christian faith vulnerable to psychological criticism. The result of this is that the Christian life becomes more problematical for many believers and, more importantly, for those with whom we wish to share the interpretative stance derived from our faith.

To become like Christ is not to become like our own (or for that matter like any other) image of him, but to take into ourselves through prayer and practice the distinctive model of the incarnation. This is not 'Jesus', but is the series of processes that we have discerned in our earlier discussion. It demonstrates that creative living is possible when we affirm limitations and risk negotiations on this basis. Through meditation we can better discern critical boundaries, chiefly through becoming increasingly alive to the major boundary between our self and God.

We are now speaking of God and the human soul. 'Soul' has largely fallen into disuse. But the word still has a distinctive and valuable use. It describes the human person viewed as the image of God. Negotiation between God and man, establishing the boundaries of the self and of God through meditation, is crucial for the survival of this dimension of our humanity.

Confronted by various assaults upon religion, belief and the Church, Christians have to a degree withdrawn from this field. As a result we have become impervious to the questions being directed at our belief by the various social sciences and, more significantly, by ordinary people whose lives have been informed by them. Christians have responded in terms of religion's personal and social usefulness. But the point of contact and thus of mutual illumination between Christian doctrine, common human experience and religious behaviour will be less in shared action, undergirded though it may be by bits of theology or Scripture, than in holding to the apparent uselessness, but essential need for all humanity, of prayer.

If, however, Christians do not sustain the model of the incarnation as the linking paradigm, they will lose the focus for their meditation and hence for their distinctive life. They will then be unable to take the opportunities which arise for interpretation of and contribution to the life of others. For even this most intimate or private religious activity carries implications for others.

The recovery of the soul may be one thing that is vitally needed today to preserve the human race. That is not the judgement of a Christian alone. Others, too, as they observe the responses that we humans make to the pressures of living in mass societies, have issued the same challenge [Bettelheim 1986]. Prayer as meditation on the model of the incarnation, therefore, is nothing less than a key means to human salvation.

b) Contemplation

Meditation focuses outwards from the self to Jesus Christ. Contemplation looks within, so that, as we pray, we become more aware of ourselves. An occasional outcome is the ecstatic wish to lose oneself and to be absorbed in Christ, which has been regarded as the height of spiritual experience. But, as we have already noted, this is inadequate as a proclamation of the Christian life. What is more, it offers no point of engagement with contemporary spiritualities. These have a quality of contemplation about them, as people seek ways of affirming a personal dimension to human life—meaning, value and purpose [Carr 1974].

In the context of that search, talk of the loss of self is incomprehensible. As the feeling and thinking agent, the self is central to the agenda and cannot be relegated to the periphery. There is little point in trying to interpret all human experience in the light of the gospel unless we are prepared to value that experience in its own right. In addition, the notion of loss of self does not accurately represent Christian contemplation. It carries overtones of merging, so that, if self-awareness is removed, somehow there is no obstacle to everything being seen as God. If one term in the encounter is absorbed into the other, then there can be no meeting. In an age when one of the searches is for personal significance and identity, it is no gospel to begin by implying that you have to lose what you seek before you have found it and had a chance to explore it.

The other side of this, which appears from time to time in the Christian tradition, is that God ceases to be needed as God, since the sum of spirituality is all self. The sublime moment of true insight is claimed to occur when we abandon God. But this approach, too, fails to engage with common human experience or with the religious experience of most. To take leave of God represents a sophistication which remains beyond the capacity of most, and is therefore doubtful as a normative experience for the religious life. The persistence of religion, too, runs counter to this trend. It still tends to add encrustation around prevailing ideas of God in some form, and shows little sign of declining. There is a theological significance to this, which cannot be ignored (see below, pp. 197—201).

Meditation alerts us to boundaries; contemplation to negotiation. In thinking about the incarnation, we saw that a series of linkings was needed to sustain the world in hope. But the profound experience which follows, when we come to see and value such connections, is one of extraordinary vulnerability. This appears wherever we turn in our reflection on these linkings. Divine vulnerability emerges in the incarnation, because there God opens himself to scrutiny. Our vulnerability is similar, when we reflect on how fragile our relations are with one another and with God. Vulnerability is not a quality added to these relations; it is intrinsic as the result of the effort that is needed to preserve their tensions and to keep them creative.

Contemplation, therefore, has a specific function. It is a consciously self-reflective act, practised in order to maintain the tension and vulnerability of that incarnation which is the object of our meditation and the model of our ministry. It is, therefore, stressful work, calling for an intellectual and emotional integrity, which is easy to think about but demanding to exercise. It is also difficult because it depends upon meditation, our focusing on the model of God's activity which is made known in Jesus. In the new context created by that prayer, Christian contemplation follows as we enter upon self-reflection, which neither denies our selves nor merely affirms them. By this means the model of the incarnation is so absorbed that it instinctively becomes the reflective stance for pastoral ministry.

Meditation and contemplation in the light of our thinking about the incarnation give the command to watch and pray (Matt. 26.41) renewed meaning. To watch is to hold the processes of the incarnation as the focus of our meditation; to pray is to sustain that model in ourselves through that contemplation in which we repeatedly negotiate between ourselves and Christ. As Christians, we pray by meditating on the limitations of our lives and their usability and by exploring various boundaries in ourselves and God.

c) Intercession

Meditation and contemplation establish the Christian's role; intercession is about making that role work. This is also another fraught area. Whether it be to save the starving in Africa by praying for rain or the profits of the village fête by praying for sun, the exercise is incredible. But the expressions of hope in each case are not meaningless. The dynamic that we perceive in the incarnation illuminates intercession and connects it with both faith and pastoral practice, whatever the persisting philosophical problems.

At the heart of the matter lies the difference between hope and hopefulness. It is today a commonplace to think of God as the end towards which all things tend. But theologies of hope are often difficult to grasp, since we do not easily distinguish general feelings of optimism or hopefulness from genuine hope — that life-sustaining stance which is engendered less from within than through effective negotiation between ourselves and our context.

Hope is the crucial issue in intercession. Through such prayer we discover again that the conscious and unconscious dynamics of our human life in relationships are not merely a given context for living. We are to understand them as an aspect of his creation with which God has deliberately engaged. Once we see that, we have a ground for working on the difference between genuine hope and fantasized hopefulness. The two are separable, but in the muddiness of human life we frequently confuse them. The tendency to idealize, which runs through our unconscious life, leads to optimism which is unrelated to reality. This sometimes emerges in religion as intercessory prayer. But if we grasp that those aspects of ourselves which produce this result can be employed for mature living, then no prayer need become mere hopefulness or fantasy. The means by which we can discern what is happening is offered by the model of the incarnation.

In intercessory praying we consciously take back into ourselves what we are part of—those relationships with God, our neighbour and ourselves that we are invited by the model of the incarnation to interpret through God's involvement in such pairs. To pray in this way sets us firmly in our role as people of God within its context of the wider world. This ceases to be populated by me and my fantasies alone—although they will be there and will be tested by the exercise. The world's realities are introduced into worship and prayer exactly at the point where we are most acutely aware of our role in relation to God. We have to articulate them, not as if we are reading the news to God, but in the confused and emotionally laden state that we are in. In intercession world issues are not outside us; they are offered as they are found inside us, whether directly, because we are immediately caught up in them, or distantly, because we are partially aware of them and their seriousness.

We cannot, therefore, intercede without evaluating our motives. But we are now, because of our reflection on the incarnation, aware that prayer on behalf of others will involve us in questioning who these others are and what they represent to and for us. They cannot be offered to God by us without our also offering our own participation, in whatever form that takes.

It might be thought, however, that such a view of intercession implies that the only change that may come about is in our perspective on ourselves. One result certainly is heightened awareness of our roles and responsibilities in the world. But such self-awareness does not benefit us alone; intercessory prayer, when seen in this light, is also a significant contribution to the well-being of others and of the world in general. For it offers a means by which altruism can be affirmed and activated.

One disabling effect of contemporary scepticism is that any altruistic stance is automatically suspect. Some argue on the basis of biology or psychology that genuine altruism is inconceivable. Self-interest will always dominate. But even if this is true in a clinical sense (and that is arguable), in common human experience altruism is necessary if people are not to degenerate into a series of self-enclosed, private and other-disregarding individuals or groups. In intercessory prayer we address in a practical way this universal question: Can one person act on behalf of another for that person's benefit and well-being? Pastoral practice, the model of the incarnation and the distinctively religious activity of prayer coincide and mutually inform each other around this question and demand a confident, but realistically based, affirmative answer.

This heightened awareness of others demonstrates the significance of intercession in the context of human relations and the classic of the incarnation. Pairing represents a primitive aspect of our unconscious selves. It seems to be a means by which we deal with a rage which may either destroy ourselves and others or be harnessed to creative partnership. This unconscious process, the detail of which does not matter here, explains many of those ambivalent feelings which we frequently experience at intercession. On the one hand we think that it is a good thing to pray for others and praying, therefore, gives us approval. Yet on the other hand, when we think objectively about it, it seems a foolish and apparently useless thing to do, and it can stimulate unadmitted anger against those who seek, or even seem to demand, our prayers.

This is one reason why there is so much unhelpful intercession in the Church's public worship. This prayer is often used by congregations and ministers alike as a way of defending themselves against their feelings of impotent anger at God for the way the world is. Because ministers and congregations are uncertain about intercession, it becomes the part of the service that anyone is allowed to do. It is divorced from the structure and detail of the worship and from the concerns which the congregation as a whole may have. An individual is left to manage this problematic piece of religious activity. And, when their attempt proves irrelevant or unhelpful, it is easier to castigate the leader, publicly or privately, than to acknowledge our own rage against a God who allows the world to be as it is and himself to be so impotent, when he is — so we at least unconsciously assume — being sustained by our worship.

The content of prayers also demonstrates this underlying wish to protect ourselves from our feelings about God. This often degenerates into self-affirming thanksgiving, stressing God's blessings to his people, and by implication disposing of others as the unblessed. At other times it becomes thinly disguised exhortation, which covers an unrecognized anger against God for the world being as it is. Because it is difficult, intercession often ceases to be prayer offered to God on behalf of all others, and degenerates into self-congratulation. It is probable, therefore, that Jesus' story about the Pharisee and the publican (Luke 18.10 — 14) was about intercession.

If, however, we can integrate this basic Christian activity with our pastoral practice and theological perception, we can face this tendency to defend ourselves and the feelings which are associated with it. By so doing we can also be enabled to move away from exclusive attitudes, which produce destructive behaviour, and begin to look at the world and ourselves in terms of co-operative, creative activity with God and with one another.

B.   To Double Business Bound: The Classic of the Atonement

———

My stronger guilt defeats my strong intent,
And like a man to double business bound
I stand in pause where I shall first begin,
And both neglect.
                    (Shakespeare, *Hamlet*, 3.3.40—43)

EIGHT

Atonement, Ambivalence and Ambiguity

Religious and common human experience coincide in the dilemmas — moral, social and spiritual — which always confront human beings. St Paul, for example, agonizes that, in spite of birth, status, faith and teaching, he finds himself willing one course of action and pursuing another (Rom. 7). He does not speak for the religious person alone; he is everyone. Job, sitting in the ashes of his life, surrounded by friends who grind him further into the dust, is not just the archetypal man of faith. He is everyone who has known the bitterness of undeserved suffering and its unremitting pressure, which reduces all comment to banality.

Our life is intrinsically insecure and uncertain. We live with ambivalence and ambiguity. These are two quintessential words of modern life. Found primarily in literary criticism and psychology, they describe a new awareness in mankind. 'Ambiguity' describes how each situation is suffused with options which are not obviously distinguishable in value. 'Ambivalence' speaks of the opposed attitudes, feelings or values which the individual may find in tension within himself, almost, but not necessarily, tearing him apart. For many these are also prominent in religious belief, which appears simultaneously important and unimportant, true but untrue, vital but unnecessary. In our ambiguous context we become ambivalent, as we grapple with the meaning of Christian commitment and behaviour.

The Dynamics of Achievement

'Ambiguity' and 'ambivalence' sound undesirable. They conjure up a picture of people who dither when decisiveness is needed. Yet the way that we handle them is the foundation of action both by individuals and organizations. One of our earliest developmental experiences is to discover that we cannot simply fall back upon presumed maternal support. We have to act, to struggle with our mother. We also learn that we cannot always reflect on ourselves and order our internal world before acting. The outside world impinges with such force that we have to respond to it and its effect on our inner world. We may, therefore, have to act, even irrationally, but at least to some effect.

The key to this side of our behaviour lies in the way that we relate to the external world. Our actions are marked by projective behaviour. This appears in the everyday experience of seeing in others faults or virtues which we cannot acknowledge in ourselves. Or, as Jesus put it, we fail to cast out the speck in our own eye before dealing with the beam in our neighbour's (Matt. 7.3—5). But although this may be a technique for defending ourselves against something which we dislike or feel to be threatening, the outcome is that we are confronted with choice. We may acknowledge that part of ourself which we are projecting on to the other and try to do something about it. Or we may split ourselves from it, leave it in the other person and try to avoid it and the associated anxieties.

Whenever there is choice there is, therefore, always a double dynamic or, in a general sense, ambivalence in us. This feeling originates in our earliest phases of development. As a baby we at first experience the world as composed of good and bad objects to which we respond by a split within ourselves, so that we love or hate. It is beyond our capacity to hold these objects and emotions at the same time. In normal development, however, we learn to do this and to cope with the range of associated feelings. The technical word 'ambivalence' refers to this ability to hold love and hate, good and bad together. But as with all human development, this is not a simple progression. We do not entirely abandon one phase as we move to the next; the primitive parts of ourselves survive, and somewhere underlying our ordinary ambivalence is to be found the violence of the earlier stage.

We also see this ambivalence in groups, where it appears as fight/flight behaviour. This is the only basic assumption

which is explicitly twofold, containing the double option—
both fight and flight. It is not divided into one or other of
these; aggressive fight or fearful flight are always simultaneous
possibilities. A group can switch with surprising speed from
one to the other. The fact that this single underlying
assumption itself contains the two possibilities reminds us
how complex this world is. We have to mobilize these
ambivalent parts of ourselves, whether individually or in a
group, in order to achieve anything. But implicitly at the
same time, because of this ambivalence, we act on the basis
of emotional uncertainty. Projective behaviour may have two
outcomes—attachment to what we project or rejection of it.
These are parallel to the dynamic of fight/flight in a group.
When one is active, the other is only temporarily obscured.

Recent converts frequently provide a clear illustration of
this phenomenon. They may rapidly become eager evangelists
as, highly motivated by new-found faith, they seek to convert
all around them, but they are also the most vulnerable to the
collapse of that belief when they come up against anything
unexpected or unfamiliar. This collapse is described in several
ways—lack of depth, shortage of experience, or needing time
to consolidate belief. But one way of seeing it is in terms of
unconscious projective behaviour, by which unresolved
tensions and anxieties in the convert's religious experience
(which is itself at an early stage) are projected on to others
and dealt with there, usually with enthusiastic aggressiveness.
Converts' behaviour is ambiguous because they have not yet
come to terms with the ambivalences that lie at the root of all
religious experience, including theirs.

When this phenomenon appears in a congregation or
committee, the double dynamic of fight/flight prevails. A
heightened sense of excitement and anxiety is coupled with
inevitable uncertainty. The behaviour of such a group, even
when the underlying dynamic is discerned, is unpredictable.

Ambiguity and the Cross

There can be no doubt which Christian classic relates to this
dynamic: it is the cross, *the* symbol of Christianity. Nothing
in the Christian faith seems more secure, it is a focus for
commitment, creating demand and support for the believer

and impressing itself upon the non-believer. Yet central though this classic is, no one doctrine of that cross has ever been promulgated as orthodox. The classics of the incarnation and Trinity have both been formulated and consolidated in creeds. By contrast, the cross and atonement have been left free from definition. The cross is central and essential. Without it there is nothing identifiably Christian. Yet its precise meaning and significance seem to have been deliberately left undefined.

Claims about the cross are also ambiguous. It is described in the same breath as victory and defeat, achievement and failure, the end of one man's delusion and the moment of salvation for all mankind. It is the persistent problem and the persistent symbol. This may explain why, as seems to happen at critical junctures in the Church's history, the generally accepted understanding of the atonement becomes unsatisfactory.

> Traditional doctrines of atonement are a source of deep dissatisfaction to almost all sensitive Christians. Their transactional character, whether expressed in terms of propitiation, substitution, or payment of a debt, make them an easy target for criticism. Yet the cross of Christ remains a powerful source of the experience of forgiveness and renewal. [Wiles 1982, 66]

This power is apparent in the two approaches to the atonement which have dominated Western thought. For almost a thousand years Christians hardly attempted a coherent doctrine. The prevailing image—an analogy or parable, rather than a theory—was of *Christus victor*, the triumphant Christ who paid a ransom for mankind's salvation. The moral problem represented by the powerful experience of oppressive evil was firmly left with God.

Subsequently, however, two main streams of development can be discerned. The first is based on Anselm's theory of satisfaction. Its weaknesses have often been identified: it reverses the biblical stance that the cross reconciled man to God, and presents a view of God as the one who needs reconciling; man becomes isolated from creation as a whole; salvation is achieved by his escaping an awesome God to find refuge in a loving Christ. The theory of penal substitution emerges, which has its own internal logic but does not work well as a metaphor, since it requires that justice becomes apparently injustice. Yet this view of the cross and atonement has enabled men and women to believe that their personal freedom and survival are guaranteed, however oppressive the forces ranged against them, and to act accordingly. The cost is felt to be borne by God in Jesus Christ, even though logically the real cost may turn out to be to God's credibility. Yet the individual's sense of being saved can be so intense that the further consequences of this theory are left unexamined. There is, therefore, something about the ambiguity of God, as he is presented in this penal theory, which serves the believer. Because the penal theory preserves the two central aspects of the cross, ambiguity and cost, it has outlasted (and still survives) the attacks made on its reasonableness or its biblical credentials.

In contrast stands the 'subjectivist' approach associated with Abelard. Beholding the cross, men and women may see the love of God poured out in Christ's death, absorb that love, and become conformed to it. The love of God displayed in the dying Christ evokes an answering love in the person who contemplates it. It is a view which has consistent power, but which is vulnerable as a theory to the general criticism that the component of justice, which is implicit in the biblical traditions about the cross, is too severely diminished. But the issue of cost re-emerges. The believer experiences salvation as a change of heart, but the cost of bringing about that change seems out of all proportion to the effect. It is too easy to think of alternative ways, and the need for the crucifixion does not remain apparent. But this view, too, has been and still is effective in generating saving love, because, although very different from Anselm's theory, it too preserves the twin essentials of the cross—ambiguity and cost.

Contemporary thinking about the cross seems to be moving back behind such theorizing. Recently the theme of sacrifice has re-emerged. Although the practice is remote from the modern world, the concept is widely used. One way in which the concept of sacrifice is employed today is through the use of the term 'scapegoat'. For example, in family therapy this word describes the member of the family who is sacrificed by the others in order to save themselves having to face aspects of their individual and social behaviour [Zinner & Shapiro 1972]. The idea of sacrifice has often lain dormant beneath the surface of social consciousness. But from time to time it re-emerges to illuminate a facet of common human experience which is in danger of being overlooked or denied [Young 1975; Young 1982]. The themes of autonomy and alienation and the sense of being abandoned by God (and abandoning him) also permeate recent reflection on mankind and the innocently dying Christ. The cross becomes the place of God's death, both in the sense of the death of the old gods of theism and the place where Jesus, and hence all mankind, experiences the death of or absence of God. The cry of dereliction resonates with much in modern art and literature. The suffering God, who shares the agonies of his creation, becomes, in spite of difficulties, a theological necessity. God not only fully experiences the ultimate human limitation—death—but also the spiritual finitude of God-abandonedness. The outcome is neither despair nor adulation, but the consequences are found in today's theological and human crises [Moltmann 1974]. In each of these themes of sacrifice and the death of God we again observe the theme of ambiguity linked with a sense of cost being publicly borne.

Throughout the history of the Christian classic of the atonement one point regularly emerges: whenever it becomes the focus for reflection, imagination or theorizing, the fact of the cross itself becomes critically active. Every meditation and theological elaboration upon the cross becomes itself scrutinized by the cross. Every theory or theology suffers a reflexive test from the cross. And we dare even suggest, with Luther, that God himself is examined by the cross: 'The cross puts everything to the test. Blessed is he who understands' [*WA* V.179.31; van Loewenich 1976]. No theory is sufficient which does not offer an idea about how salvation is achieved and at what cost. The classic of the cross and atonement is about achievement, and some criteria of what that is have to be incorporated in any understanding. Moreover, the ambiguous nature of the cross is effective for others only in so far as it questions itself. And it is intrinsic to the cross that, while explanation must be attempted, it remains inexplicable and unexplained. When any theological interpretation seems to diminish that ambiguity, even if for a time it seems clear and powerful, it too eventually comes under judgement. Those, therefore, who are to be saved through the cross of Christ must be allowed to be conscious of their own ambivalent feelings and attitudes towards this symbol.

We can clarify this general observation into four major issues which arise from reflection upon this Christian classic.

Four Issues in the Classic of the Atonement

First, every theory of the cross and the atonement must have inadequacy built into it. This may arise from a particular cultural conditioning. The ransom view, for example, relies upon a specific stance towards Scripture; Anselm's interpretation depends to a large extent upon the social structures of his age; Abelard's reacts against the prevailing theologies that he was required to teach; Young, from her profound experience as a mother, demonstrates the renewed cultural context for sacrifice; and Moltmann responds to the contemporary crisis of identity and relevance which he discerns.

It is beyond question that views of the cross are culturally conditioned; but it is noticeable that they are not culturally confined. The drawing power of penal theories persists in spite of social changes. Abelard's stance still attracts because of the perennial beauty of human intimacy and love. Even sacrifice, which has little obvious connection with today's world, can come alive. Of all the Christian classics, the cross is the most culturally conditioned and historically located. The crucifixion is set in history and culture in a way that incarnation, creation and resurrection are not, and the once-for-all character of the atonement is notable. Yet this cross is the distinctive Christian symbol and forms the continuing point of judgement on all in every age that claims status as Christian.

Second, the Church has been unwilling to define an official doctrine of the atonement. This is not only an effect of the cross on Christian practice and theology, but also demonstrates the evangelical mode of the gospel of the cross. St Paul claimed that 'we preach Christ and him crucified' (1 Cor. 1.23); alternatively the cross may be presented as the means of religious, cultural or political revolution. But in each way the cross is the distinctive demand of the gospel. Because it addresses the world at large, and the Christian community specifically, the cross cannot endure being overlaid with theory, and the Church's instinct to resist endorsing one theory witnesses to this critical function.

Third, the cross is always associated with a specific achievement. It may be that the world is changed, the radical disjunction of sin is overcome, or sacrifice is effectively ordered, but all emphasize achievement through the cross. The phrase 'the work of Christ' usually refers to his passion and death, even though a sounder theological stance would apply it to the whole range of his incarnation, life, death and resurrection. But even in that larger context the cross and passion are the fulcrum on which the arguments turn, or the lens through which the other aspects of Christ are given clear reference and meaning.

Fourth, there is the matter of pain and suffering. No interpretation which lessens or removes the reality of Christ's suffering and death has survived for long. The reality of his suffering has repeatedly been reaffirmed in three ways. Firstly, by noting that Jesus experienced physical pain like any other victim of a crucifixion. The Gospels do not minimize this, and the imagery has proved rich for art and devotion. At times of disenchantment with theology this aesthetic view has sustained the cross at the centre of Christian belief, life and devotion. Secondly, by perceiving the suffering associated with sin. All theories of the atonement are concerned with sin and forgiveness. The need to make amends for faults or the wish for cleansing in the face of divine purity are taken into the death of Christ. The arguments are about the means; the end is not disputed. When a highly personalized sense of sin is explored, the intense experience of guilt is also related closely to the cross. This accounts for the continuing attraction of the satisfaction and substitutionary theories. Although the precise means by which the death of Christ deals with man's guilt may remain unclear, the experience of liberation or salvation is such that inconsistencies in the doctrine are tolerated. Thirdly, by a recognition that pain and suffering involve cost. Here the isolation of the cross from its theological context can prove dangerous. Devotion to the passion and to images of purely human suffering can become morbidly narcissistic. Yet a strong sense of cost is crucial to any awareness of the cross, theoretical, emotional or aesthetic, and nowhere is this more evoked than in meditation on the pain and suffering inflicted.

The four issues in the classic of the atonement indicate the essential ambiguity of the cross. There is a tension in two directions, which, if resolved in favour of either, the fact of the cross itself immediately reintroduces: it is the core of the Church's proclamation, but it is also the stumbling-block of the gospel.

The Felt Atonement

The term 'mystery' may be too easily used in connection with the cross. But it points us in the right direction, since mysteries are felt, not understood. The classic of the cross and atonement, too, cannot be considered apart from the various feelings of those involved, both then in the story and now through belief. The gospel narratives put physical and psychological feelings at the core of their accounts. In the passion narratives the people who surround Jesus become rounded characters. Up to that point we have been given evidence for the Kingdom of God, which is disclosed through nameless lepers, an anonymous young ruler or an unknown Syrophoenician woman — interesting people whose faith and responses to Jesus contribute to our identifying who he is and maybe even in some way to his own self-discovery. We inevitably speculate about them, but we have little information or detail.

By contrast, however, as the passion story begins the characters become named, feeling people: Pilate and his wife; the priests and their human jealousies; Joseph and his secret faith; Peter and Judas; even an unimportant servant, Malchus, develops a name and role in the tradition. It is as if we now must have fully human beings in their own right. The sense of mystery which we associate with the cross arises from an instinctive sense that, as these people, with their passions, uncertainties, desires and feelings, become so much more evidently human beings, then, when we think of God's own involvement in this event, we may be nudging what may riskily be termed 'the feeling side of God'.

This point has recently been reaffirmed in contemporary

theologies of the crucified God. Moltmann, for example, following Luther, points out that the primary function of Christ's cross is discernment of reality. Since 'the test of everything is the cross', the 'everything' includes the question 'What does the cross of Jesus mean for God himself?' as part of the question of what the cross means for humankind, in particular for me [Moltmann 1974, 201].

A similar vein runs through reflection of a less theologically sophisticated kind. It is, therefore, wise to trust instinct, and inquire about the implications of such thought. For instance, the apparent conflict between the so-called subjective and objective theories of the atonement diminishes. Feelings expressed in devotion to the crucified one have instinctively refused to admit a distinction. Meditation and contemplation, as we earlier saw, complement each other. This is especially true of meditation on the crucified one and the self-awareness that follows through contemplation. The reason for this may lie in the way in which the classic of the atonement raises the level of our consciousness of and questioning about the feeling side of God as this is displayed in the crucified Christ. Matching feelings are generated in ourselves, and the distinction between his 'objective' work and our 'subjective' response ceases to feel significant.

These double or ambivalent feelings, with which God involves himself in the classic of the atonement, are powerful and frequently confusing. But they also represent the part of ourselves which we have to harness for any achievement. They are powerful because they originate within the earliest phase in our development as human beings, the psychological bedrock of who we are. But without these primitive emotions and the managing of chaotic experience into some sort of order — the acknowledgement of ambivalence — we should not possess the facets of a human existence which produce results. These include all the risky aspects of life — creating an attitude of healthy suspicion and questioning, forming ideals, and sustaining the effort to act.

To achieve anything we have to deal with the world outside us, which we might regard as 'objective'. But as we do so, we become increasingly aware that it is not all 'out there'. We are handling our internal worlds, too, or what we might label the 'subjective' aspect to life. We, therefore, become anxious about both our inner selves and the outside world. Interaction between them is necessary for any achievement, but it is also implicitly dangerous. But the more aware we become of that, the more our anxiety increases. Sometimes it becomes too much, and we revert to the comforting debilitation of dependence.

The gospel story of Jesus' agony in the Garden of Gethsemane provides a fine illustration of this interaction. The choices before Jesus lie between fight (which the disciple with the sword acts out on behalf of everyone) and flight (in which finally all the disciples indulge). Their behaviour is that of a group locked into feelings alone, what we might call basic assumption-based behaviour, and is unable to harness them to some useful purpose. As a result the disciples collapse into childlike dependence upon Jesus at just the moment when he is least likely to be able to respond effectively. Anxiously they look to him to resolve the problems and doubts which increasingly press on them just when he is most occupied with his own self and his response to external circumstances. As a result, all the actions in the Garden, instead of achieving something positive, act like lightning conductors to remove power from all. The disciples' dependence is focused upon Jesus, and when he fails to meet their expectations of powerful leadership through divine intervention, they are lost. He is left alone to explore what that fight and flight and the feelings of ambivalence and ambiguity mean — ultimately crucifixion.

The account also suggests that Jesus has prepared himself for this in his earlier praying. Struggling with God he realizes that, if he himself shifts into that dependent mode of behaviour and surrenders his responsibility for his actions to God, nothing will be achieved. So we are told of ambivalence in his praying; he is caught between unconsidered surrender to God (dependent behaviour) and the taking of a responsible decision to do what is necessary (harnessing his dependence upon God to the task in hand). A deepening awareness dawns that, if he continues to harness the prevailing feelings for his work, then there will be casualties, chief among which may be his intimacy with God, but that this may be the cost of achievement.

This is precisely what Christians find in their reflection on the cross. Both in the theological tradition and in our own experience it resists every attempt at understanding, whether religious, cultic, mystical or ethical, because each diminishes its stark horror. They divert attention from feelings to believed understanding, as people demand that God be the God they wish him to be: one who escapes crucifixion. In the story of Gethsemane the disciples act out this resolution of basic anxiety while Jesus supports the ambivalence. Similarly in the history of Christian spirituality there has been pressure to soften the reality of the cross by inviting God to accede to our dependent wish not to be involved. But through the persistent theme of the uninterpretable cross God protects the necessary ambivalence of fight/flight against the pressures towards dependence.

The Transaction of the Cross, Evil and Guilt

The problems of evil and guilt focus in the cross. The idea of a devil has been used to keep evil apart from God. This is the core, for example, of the classic idea of *Christus victor*. Alternatively evil may be reduced to personal sin and in the mysticism of the cross handled through private meditation, confession and absolution. But at the end of the twentieth century neither type of approach is tolerable in the face of the scale of actual evil which our generation experiences.

The question is so large that any attempt to interpret seems to trivialize it. Casual Christian discussion of intolerable evil in the light of the cross tends to be vapid; it also finds itself under the judgement of that cross. One means, however, by which today's Christian pastor can begin to approach this massive dimension to human life, without losing touch with the reality of evil or the theological and spiritual significance of the cross of Christ, is by reflecting on recent Jewish experience. This exercise is not novel; the first Christians did something similar when they appropriated the Old Testament. Today's equivalent is to take recent Jewish experience as data.

By 'experience' Jewish writers mean 'interpreted feeling'. Contemplating the Nazi attempt to exterminate the Jews in Europe, a conclusion has to be reached. It is not enough merely to record the raw data, which we might call 'the experience'. Interpretation of some sort is needed so that profound emotions can be integrated with reflection and so become distinctively 'Jewish'. This leads to a series of competing standpoints—the dying Jews were atoning on behalf of mankind's sins; the camps were the place of God's revelation, where he reaffirmed his faithfulness to the covenant; God ceased to exist after Auschwitz; or the whole episode is another instance of the unknowable plan of an inscrutable God. But the crucial problem is faced by all: the problem of evil requires a struggle with God. They raise the questions about God, the scale of evil, and the atonement which contemporary Christianity must address [Simon 1967], although no Christian may presume to decide between these approaches. The choice lies starkly between the cross (or the Holocaust, which itself means—'great sacrifice') as the place where the window opens upon God or where he finally denies himself.

The image of a window is worth elaborating. A window forms part of a wall, letting the light in and allowing people to look through the wall. When a window is incorporated, a wall ceases to be a barrier between us and the outside world; it becomes a boundary across which transactions can be effected. Through it we look out at the world outside. We do not enter that world, but bring it through the clear glass across the boundary of the wall into our inside world.

When considering God and the problem of evil, we can regard the cross as such a window. Through it God's internal world draws into itself what seems separate from or outside him—that is, evil at its most excruciatingly powerful and inscrutable. At the same time the cross also opens up the inside world of God to those caught up in and dominated by so much evil. He invites us to see him making this awesome 'other' world of evil his own. This is where the traditional idea of transaction, which is associated with atonement, fits.

Transaction between God and evil (however precisely that is defined) lies deep in the classic of the atonement. It has proved, however, to be a focal point around which fantasy has most easily developed. In this field, where imagination reigns, powerful images in art, drama and music have been produced. They have stimulated and sustained belief and guided the way that people think and live. But with the psychoanalytic developments of our century the world of fantasy has been examined and exposed, and we are less confident in it than were our predecessors. However, this is no reason for abandoning the significance of fantasy; we need to consider the modern contributions to its understanding and see what they may add to our theological reflection.

Fantasy is not a whim or an eccentricity. It may contain elements of wish-fulfilment, but it is more than that. At one time 'fantasy' was frequently contrasted with 'reality' and its value diminished accordingly. Now, however, we begin again to realize that the world of fantasy and the 'real' world are not opposed. We construct our world through the interplay of both, just as we live in the interaction of conscious and unconscious minds. Fantasy, therefore, is an important factor in our existence.

Unexamined fantasies, however, tend to undermine the significance of the issue that they are being generated to handle. For example, even if we operate with a less personalized notion of evil than is implied by the title 'devil', it may be so fantasized as to be assigned a matching status with God. Christian thought is prone to this sort of dualism. Not surprisingly, therefore, the devil has an uncanny knack of emerging as a more attractive, more competent and usually more powerful figure than God himself. Yet instinctively through worship and through use of Scripture and the Christian tradition we sense that this is not just a theological error. Something more profound is out of joint. While we may have moments in which we surrender hope, the tradition in which we stand and the better moments in our experience assert that the world is not simply evil. Or, as we might say, a fantasy which has developed for good reason (the experience of evil) has lost touch with reality, in this case God, in whom the Christian trusts.

The issue, however, is more complex. Evil is enormous, but it so resonates with the small worlds of our selves that, in order to comprehend it, we instinctively feel we have to locate it in some being who is beyond redemption, whether a supremely evil man or a devil. But at the same time such evil cannot be easily personalized, since it seems to be on such a cosmic scale that it overwhelms our idea of what is personal, including even God himself. To think about evil at all, therefore, we need fantasy. This may explain the impressive range of imagery that accrues around the figure of a devil and why the idea of transaction has so often been focused upon him. When living with fantasy, we always need to discover reality, whatever the difficulty and the cost. If atonement, the reintegration of all creation, is to come about, we must be able to recognize reality both in our notion of God and of what he deals with. Most of the post-Auschwitz Jewish theologians have grasped this on our behalf: either their various conceptions of God have to be abandoned or the reality of the evil (represented by the Holocaust) has to be perceived as a specific manifestation of God.

Transaction in the atonement, therefore, is not between God and some other figure, such as the devil. It is between God, in his role as the Creator of this world, and the fundamental realities of that creation, which are our experience of it – pain, suffering, evil and death. These cannot be diminished in importance or set aside. They are among the products of God's self-giving in creation. Simplistic imagery which creates a devil to solve this tension is merely fantasy. Evil ceases to be any particular person's responsibility – mine, the devil's or God's. As such, while it may give momentary relief, it cannot address the awesome reality of pain and suffering in a world where we are now all victims.

The transaction in the atonement occurs between God and himself. All transactions include common marks. By this process people jointly create something new and in which they invest themselves; it is marked by movement as the parties give and receive; and it is not an end itself but brings about change. Each of these characteristics is discernible in the atonement. God does not struggle with something (evil) or someone (the devil) other than himself, inviting us to join in disposing of our sin, evil and guilt into that object or being. Instead, in the cross God acknowledges a profound reality of the world which he has created, accepting it as his responsibility along with the associated pain and suffering.

The basis of atonement lies in the freedom of his creatures, for which on the cross God takes public responsibility. The gospel stories of the crucifixion all give this freedom prominence. Peter is free to stay faithful to Jesus or deny him, and he decides; Judas is free to betray his leader and to commit suicide; Pilate, Caiaphas, the crowd, the soldiers, and the disciples are all given permission to act autonomously. Although in each Gospel Jesus, as he moves to Jerusalem, generates a sense of destiny, there is scarcely a hint that the participants in the drama lose their freedom to be and do what they wish. They are allowed, indeed encouraged, to exercise it freely. The cumulative effect is the cross. Freedom does not belong to individuals alone. Each actor is caught up in wider networks than he or she knows, but that fact does not take away their responsibility for their own actions, some of which are mistaken and which induce guilty feelings [Rivkin 1986].

Guilt consists of the feelings which result from the exercise of our responsibility. Sometimes these feelings become very confused and we slide into a pathological state which rightly requires treatment. But a sense of guilt is not necessarily unfortunate or morbid, needing to be removed or explained away. It is the inevitable corollary of the exercise of our freedom as human beings. Such felt guilt, therefore, is a prerequisite of responsible action.

We can now begin to identify that for which God takes responsibility in the cross. The Christian proclamation often implies that there God takes upon himself responsibility for everything and everyone. But that line of argument leads to the charge that Christianity glorifies God only at the expense of human dignity. If without consulting me God assumes responsibility for what is genuinely my concern (and for which from time to time I properly feel guilty), then the charge is just. The loss of responsibility may remove the sense of guilt, but it does so at the expense of my self-esteem and value as a being created and affirmed by God himself. Salvation then proves delusory. The other result of this implicit devaluing of what is human is a Christianity which reduces the vast dimension of human pain by comparing it with the sufferings of Christ. In my morbid moments I can then believe that in some fashion I, because of my slight anguishes, can identify with him. There is no gospel here for a world which is psychologically aware, if not always psychologically sophisticated.

In the cross God acknowledges his responsibility for the *context* within which our freedom to choose is made possible and for the *fact* that this choice is open to us. He does not deprive us of the responsibility which we feel and know to be ours or of the sense of guilt that accompanies any failure to exercise it. But by publicly proving responsible for the fact and possibility of human freedom, he provides a reference point outside our human condition by which we can orientate our confused sense of guilt and thus break the inexorable cycle of despair.

Like looking through a window, we participate in the drama of the cross, whatever its theological interpretation, by watching. It thus serves as a point for constructive confession. As Hamlet remarked, there is an intimate connection between observation and drama, guilt and confession:

> I have heard
> That guilty creatures sitting at a play
> Have by the very cunning of the scene
> Been struck so to the soul that presently
> They have proclaimed their malefactions.
> (*Hamlet* 2. 2.586 – 90)

We are invited by the drama of the cross, which inhibits too much extensive theorizing about it, to confess those feelings of guilt and inadequacy which in our reflective moments oppress us. We are also offered a specific place in the context of God's overall activity where we can locate this turmoil. Confession, therefore, is not a generalized attitude towards a generally available God. It is given specific shape and content by being located in the God of the cross of Christ.

We can now better identify the transaction in the cross. We are not invited there to surrender to God our freedom as creatures and our consequent responsibility for our failures and successes, our sin and guilt. Nor does he somehow lift that responsibility from us. If that were so, the cross could drive us only to ultimate despair, since it would deprive us of our status as creatures. This is, incidentally, why some preaching of the cross has short-term effectiveness. It panders to the dependent longings of the inadequate, who seek relief from realities about themselves or about the world in which they are set. Such a gospel may be occasionally beneficial; but it will not save those who are sensitive to their autonomy and responsibility, even if they do not realize that these are gifts of the Creator God. On the cross, by contrast, God accepts the consequences of our exercise of the freedom which he has assigned us—the fact and content of our freedom as creatures.

What emerges from this act of atonement is transformed freedom. Our human bias (or sin) is to assume that our autonomy or freedom originates in ourselves. We treat it as a right or possession belonging to each of us, but in practice most of all to those who loudly claim it. But after the cross freedom can no longer be a casually exercised right, with the unexpected consequences of a sense of confusion and guilt. These feelings remain, but instead of being parts of human existence to be explained or removed, they become the avenue to a new quality of life. From being destructive, or at best unfortunate, by-products of human responsibility, they become the focal point of new creative possibilities. Since human beings are freed from having to feel responsible for the fact that they are responsible, they can confidently take authority for their lives and the consequences of their behaviour. In brief, they can afford to risk being wrong because they know that they are forgiven. New and unpredictable results ensue when such authority is exercised.

Reconciliation Through the Cross

A window, however, like a transaction, works in two directions. If the cross exposes to us the origins of our freedom in God, it also allows us to perceive how God takes into his inner life the cost of this gift. Any effective action involves cost, and the classic of the atonement is above all about achievement or salvation. The cross suggests that the cost of this is nothing less than that of God's being pulled apart.

Can we speak in any sense of God being torn apart in the cross? And if we can, is this legitimate? The second question, at least, is answered by two of the synoptic writers. Matthew and Mark both hint that it is, in the cry of desolation, 'My God, my God, why have you forsaken me?' (Mark 15.34; Matt. 27.46). Luke and John, who omit this anguished question, describe Jesus' life as ending with a gasp or a cry. But these are only indicators and suggestions. If we are to take our question about God seriously, taking licence from the Gospels themselves, we must consider what splitting represents.

One means by which we deal with what is unfamiliar, and so disturbing or difficult to handle, is by separating ourselves from it. For example, we identify others as 'them' over against 'us'. Black and white, worker and boss, men and women — these are today's obvious instances. We can hear this splitting, even in the most apparently conciliatory language, when a group of people is referred to as 'they' or 'them'. Under our many sophistications we still tend to revert to an idea of a world which is divided simplistically into good and evil in order to cope with its impossible absurdities. For example, the idea of 'state terrorism' has recently been proposed precisely to overcome the underlying belief that there are two sorts of action — governmental, which is always legitimate, and terrorist, which is totally illegitimate.

The central argument of this book is that, when God engages with human beings, he includes encounter at the unconscious level. One characteristic of that is this splitting. This behaviour, whether in an individual or a group, is not a form of debilitating weakness. It is a basic characteristic of human beings, a defence which we deploy usually in the face of imminent overwhelming stress or destructive anxiety. It is the way we are made. Now we may consider what it means in these terms for God to take responsibility for the world that he has created.

Whatever else evil is, it is other than God. Even if it is not personalized into a devil, it stands for that which is not God. The cross, however, demonstrates two points. First, it endorses this splitting as a fundamental characteristic of God's created world. No one is immune from it, and God himself affirms this givenness of what he has made by facing the pain of being pulled between what is me (God) and not-me (evil). But the process is transformed. Instead of its being a defensive projection, God on the cross transforms such splitting into yet another means of creation.

Human responsibility and its free exercise are aspects of God's gracious self-giving. They are assigned to us, not owned. When, however, we act on that freedom, the inescapable consequences are sin (failure) and evil (damage to ourselves and others) both on the individual and on the corporate scale. So when in the cross we observe God publicly taking his responsibility for the fact and content of our freedom, he also receives the destructiveness of evil and sin.

When projective behaviour is pointed out to us in everyday life, we feel guilty for having failed ourselves to perceive what we were doing. We wonder why we did it in the first place and how best to act in the light of our new perception. This anxiety may restart the defensive process, leading to yet another split between what we will acknowledge as ours and what we project into some other. At this level of fundamental psychological functioning there is an inevitability which can lead to a sense of hopelessness. A cycle seems to be set up, from which escape is impossible. We may seek solace or salvation in greater knowledge, but this rarely seems to be effective. For ourselves, let alone for our neighbour, understanding does not necessarily produce forgiveness.

Here, however, human experience illuminates the classic of the atonement. What is for us a defensive stance is given status as a creative consequence of the freedom which God gives us. We tend to deal with the destructive sin and matching guilt, which result from its exercise, thus splitting them from ourselves and projecting them into others. By contrast, however, in the cross God holds such splitting within himself and demonstrates how it becomes a means of redemption. The damaging effects are faced, not denied, and thus transformed. It is not that they do not occur for God or that they cease to matter. If this were the case, evil and sin would not hold the awesome reality for us that they do. Their power lies in their being apparently associated inevitably with the creative sides of ourselves, our freedom and autonomy.

Reflecting on this wrenching apart, our approach to the problem of evil is also transformed. The human tendency is to separate evil from good, using criteria derived from whatever belief system we adopt. It is almost intolerable to think of evil as anything other than the opposite of good. The cross, however, as the focus for all that is both good and evil, does not countenance this. It is both God's act on behalf of his creation (which is good) and at the same moment the destruction of God's righteous one (which is evil). Thus evil is affirmed for what it is. There is no magical conversion of evil into good, but in all its horror and starkness it is incorporated into God's action.

As is often the case, a gospel story illuminates these profound issues. In this case the enigma of Judas is a prime illustration of this process. Those who compiled the Gospels seem to have been sensitive to this theological dimension to the saga. Judas is not prominent as a bad object, although he could easily have been so presented, as later Christian traditions show. Abuse of him in the Gospels is minimal. On the other hand, the evil, that is the massive destructiveness for himself and others, in his actions is not underrated. Interestingly it is Judas' essentially human quality, neither absolutely evil nor determinedly responsible, but rather confused, misled and ultimately tragically mistaken, that ensures his place in the gospel narratives. The whole drama of salvation from the human perspective is encapsulated in him. That is why subsequent Christians have found themselves ambivalent about him. He is so easy an object on to which to project our own guilt, especially in relation to God, and then to dismiss. Yet at the same time, without Judas and his actions, we are without hope of salvation, since he is quintessentially in his dilemma and actions every human being. Each of us, therefore, must in the end answer the question: Can Judas be saved?

Judas' story concerns evil. There is, however, also a link between this and guilt. Underlying the issue of guilt is the central problem of authority and its exercise. To take authority is a complex act. It involves both accepting the person that I am and working in the roles, many as they are, that I hold. As a concept, therefore, authority defines all that we call human: who we are; what we are; and what we are for. When we exercise authority we feel a struggle within ourselves and may come into conflict with others. The two usually go hand in hand. Concealed, therefore, in the suffering, pain, sin and guilt which are taken up in the Christian classic of the cross and atonement, there remains the basic human fault — divinely assigned and humanly accepted authority and the perpetual problems of its exercise.

If Judas' story illuminates the problem of evil for each of us, that of the rest of the disciples, notably Peter, illustrates the connection between guilt and authority. In various ways each fails to sustain the role of disciple, which Jesus assigned them and which each accepted. But the confused welter of guilty feelings which emerge in the post-crucifixion stories is not minimized or obliterated: they are transformed. The disciples know themselves forgiven and reconciled to God, in spite of their ambivalence about him in the crucifixion. In turn this experience, first embodied in these men and women, subsequently becomes the foundation upon which the whole Christian enterprise is built.

The disciples are classic instances of all who wrestle with the guilt and splits that result from our failure to live competently with the authority which is ours as human beings. Here lies the basis of forgiveness which has always been found in the cross. It is offered in the classic of the atonement, through which we discover that forgiveness comes about in an unexpected way. Our natural inclination is to think of it as divine forgetfulness, to let the past go and, as we say, to forgive and forget. But the atonement demonstrates that forgiveness is explicitly found in remembering.

Honest remembrance is a specific instance of exercising our authority. It requires us to acknowledge our past and what has contributed to our being who we are. But we also have to recollect and examine our behaviour in role, and so confess as much guilt as we can recognize. This on its own might become morbid. But because of the forgiveness available through the atonement, our honest remembrance ceases to be a reason for despair and new hopes emerge. That is another way of talking of forgiveness. It comes about because it is rooted in realities about ourselves as human beings and in the inner reality of God himself. The primitive urge to split in order to save ourselves is ineradicable. But when this facet of his human creation is taken by God into himself, as we see at the cross, then it is transformed from a defence to an acknowledged reality to be used for constructive living.

The cross pulls together many strands of our common human experience. But it is not just a generalized symbol of the fraught nature of human life; it is the identifiable place where God publicly aligns himself with his creature. The pain, which is so central a theme of the cross, is not undeserved pain which derives from sin or guilt which do not belong to him. Nor is it just a comforting expression of solidarity with the pain of suffering and oppressed humanity. Both ideas are rich and powerfully suggestive, stimulating spiritual development and inspired action. Ultimately, however, they do not impinge upon common human experience at a sufficiently profound level for the cross to be God's saving activity for *all* his creatures. For, as any pastor knows, many people do not feel oppressed and not all live with a profound sense of sin and guilt. If the pain of the cross is to be a factor in the salvation of all men and women, it cannot be linked to only one fragment of the experience of some. Now, however, we see that in the cross God aligns himself with the fundamental experience of life which is common to us all — the evil and guilt inevitably linked with our exercise of our authority as human beings, which derives from our being creatures within God's creation.

Substitution and Representation

One further theme in this classic remains to be noted — the representative nature of the death of Christ. 'Substitution' still causes lively controversy and must be considered in any account of the atonement. As Pannenberg remarks:

> In social life, substitution is a universal phenomenon, both in conduct and in its outcome . . . If substitution is not a universal phenomenon in human social relationships, if the individualistic interpretation of responsibility and recompense need not be rejected as one-sided because it overlooks the social relationships of individual behavior, then it is not possible to speak meaningfully of a vicarious character to the fate of Jesus Christ. [Pannenberg 1968, 268]

Even if Christ's death is unique and distinctive, it must nevertheless have a vicarious effect. Otherwise it remains yet one more example of a tragic and unjustified death, albeit one which has shaped much of Western culture. To invite people to observe, meditate upon and use in the ordering of their lives the horror of one crucifixion appears selfish and hollow. Representation, therefore, is an essential theme to be retained at the heart of the classic of the atonement.

Today, however, in this respect, as in many others, we lack a conceptual framework with which to make sense of vicarious suffering and death. The process of rejecting any such notion began at the Enlightenment and, although some Christians still resist it, it has reached fruition in our present age. Mankind's horrendous record in this century, compounded by widespread knowledge of it, has had a profound impact equally on Christian theological study and pastoral sensitivity [Simon 1967; Wilkinson 1978; Wilkinson 1986]. We can, however, sustain a genuine sense of substitution if we conceive representation as a function within a relationship. In relationships people do not substitute for each other in the sense of replacement. But they do act on behalf of one another and so represent, or appropriately substitute for, one another.

For example, a marriage or a family works well so long as the participants are willing to be allowed to act on behalf of each other and, what is more difficult, are also prepared to delegate responsibility to one another and, when necessary, to others beyond their immediate circle. For instance, parents have to allow others to represent aspects of themselves to their children—teachers, to whom they delegate important learning; doctors, who are given responsibility for health; or baby-sitters, entrusted with the child's security. Indeed a grasp of this is a sign of maturity both in the individuals concerned and in the growth of the family unit itself. For it shows that we are sufficiently confident in ourselves and others to be able to entrust aspects of ourselves to them.

But the next step in delegation is more delicate and consequently more hazardous and difficult to accept. We also have to become sufficiently assured to be able to allow others to take aspects of ourselves without our permission. This is far from controlled or managed delegation; it is surrender of control. This comes about when we can recognize that we may unwittingly be asked to do things on behalf of another (or, as it is more pejoratively described, that we may be used) *and remain content with being so used.* We accept that we are objects for other people's projections, and that people are acting on them; that roles, which have not been negotiated, are being attributed to us; and, put brutally, that we are more than likely being manipulated. This is not a comfortable form of substitution, but it is an integral part of social and personal life.

This theme also lies at the heart of the classic of the atonement. The substitutionary aspect of Christ's death is not that he takes mankind's place in general or mine in particular. For many people, perhaps most, such an idea is at best difficult and, even worse, immoral. It deprives us of that responsibility which we discover in many contexts is central to our human existence. So, far from bringing life, this sort of proposed atonement actually brings death. But the cross stands consistently for divine willingness to be used and to accept the corollaries of misuse and abuse. This is one outcome of the abandonment of the defence of splitting and its transformation into a creative stance. Assigned roles, over which there is no chance to negotiate, are accepted. This does not, however, imply mere passivity. That can give, and has at times given, rise to a pathetic Christianity marked more by masochism than mission. Accepting roles generated by the projections of others still allows opportunity for their being identified, responded to and so interpreted. In the case of the cross that interpretation is not just in terms of the attempts at doctrinal understanding which have gone on since the first days. It is also a function of that starkness of the cross itself, whatever image of it we create, which we noted at the opening of this chapter.

When we see substitution in terms of such willingness to be used, however unjust and improper the use, we are offered an effective way by which there is hope of reconciliation, or constructive interrelating, between people and between mankind and God. This is what the classic of the cross and atonement affirms: to follow the way of the cross is to accept responsibility for the evil and guilt which results from my life as myself and in my roles and, even more, for the fact that I am usable by others, whether wittingly or unwittingly, and to endure the consequent cost. Here the bridge between the cross and the continuing ministry of atonement is found. For use, abuse and misuse are definitions of a ministry which embodies and thus makes present the way of the cross.

Conclusion

The felt experiences of human life seem to coincide in the ultimately indefinable classic of the atonement: it is unfair, unjust and rationally indefensible; the reason for enduring is not for any benefit to the self, but on behalf of, or for the benefit of, others; and the cost is borne, usually undeservedly, by someone other than the one to whom it seems to belong; but, and most importantly, all this does not remove the responsibility from anyone for being human, for being God's creature in his world. It is a means of enabling such life to emerge, where previously it has been obscured or repressed. Rooted in the realities of human life and behaviour and their unconscious aspects, this atonement genuinely offers salvation. Change, or conversion, does not require us first to deny what we are—human beings made in the image of God, with the authority to act and the need to co-operate with him and one another.

The atonement can thus be interpreted congruently with its tradition as a Christian classic and integrated with the demands of contemporary life and experience. Much modern theological writing on the cross is devoted to the history of the doctrine or treats the atonement as a sub-division of the incarnation. The danger in such stances is that the debate steadily moves away from the arena of everyday belief and unbelief. Even doxological theology, which takes as its ground the Christian experience and tradition of worship, seems to leave a large gap around the atonement, preferring to approach the person and significance of Christ by other routes. Yet the cross is the distinctive symbol of Christianity, and it is to the cross that Christian faith continually turns in practice, not least in the two dominical sacraments. It is, therefore, vital for Christian belief and practice that a way of integrating the cross with current appreciations of common human experience be found, if the gospel is to continue to commend itself.

NINE

Atonement and Pastoral Care

The classic of the atonement is rightly judged by how effective it is in bringing salvation to men and women. This has often been described in terms of benefits received. Through his death Christ earns benefits for mankind — eternal life, a new way of living, an intimate relationship with him, or release from the burden and consequences of sin. In today's world, however, this idea is suspect. We are less certain about motivation than our predecessors and are acutely sensitive in personal and pastoral relationships to the question. For whose benefit actually is this work? Is it genuinely for the 'client', or is the minister or counsellor constructing and enjoying an 'ego-trip'?

To resonate with today's human experience a doctrine of the atonement has to be less concerned with benefit than with involvement. Relationships raise questions of whether we can trust ourselves to one another. The experience of salvation in this setting is what we can only describe as being taken into the mystery of God. This description may sound insufficiently down-to-earth and so cause us to hesitate because of the obvious connection between mystery, mysticism and fantasy. But the more we examine the cross from the major perspective of our age (namely our awareness of our human behaviour), the more we see it as an invitation to encounter God and the transcendent dimension of life at hitherto unperceived depths. He is not, as it were, laid out on a couch for us to examine. This is not the vulnerability of the cross. It is that God exercises his responsibility for creation, for mankind, but above all, for himself publicly. Such action does not add something to what men and women already are. Rather, by being invited to peer through the window of the cross, we are freed from any need to assume a role — saint or sinner, dependent or autonomous — in order to contact God.

He invites us here to acknowledge the one role which we have been assigned by virtue of our creation — human beings. None have to transform themselves before they can be transformed by the cross.

Transgression and Reconciliation

Pastoring is frequently described as 'a ministry of reconciliation'. The phrase is grand, but is sometimes weak in content, drifting into a bland wish that personal relations or communication within an organization should be better. Drawing people together then becomes an end in itself. But this lacks theological realism and rigour; there is no clear purpose, ambivalence and ambiguity are discounted, and little is achieved, though much is justified. But achievement lies at the root of the human dynamic to which the atonement principally relates. Pastoral practice informed by this classic is likely to be very purposeful.

The vague sense of reconciliation arises when we underestimate transgression. Anselm's old judgement remains apposite to many views of God's action in the incarnation and atonement: 'You have not yet taken sufficient account of the significance of sin.' 'Transgression' is a rich word, making explicit the sense of movement that is implicit in every notion of sin. Where these notions become codified, the pastor loses contact with human reality. But when transgression is seen as movement, the underlying ambiguities and ambivalences, which are the condition for atonement, emerge.

People need to transgress, first to live and subsequently to develop. Our earliest move may be away from assumptions about our mother. Later we embark on adventures, some of which pay off and some of which do not. The first drink or the first kiss can open the way to responsible flowering as a growing adult or be the first step on the road to perdition. Christian moralists have sometimes claimed to be more sure of the direction of that step than is possible. Every such experiment is ambiguous and stirs up ambivalence in us. These moves also involve violence. This may appear as a rejection of our upbringing as we challenge home and parental influence. Or it may be seen as an attack on the accepted ideas and principles by which we have hitherto lived. We then become personally disturbed and unsure of ourselves. Such aggression, towards ourselves or others, is nevertheless essential, since without this type of fight we do not become anything at all. The pastor regularly meets both types of person: those who have committed some transgression and are anxious about having done it and about its consequences; and those who need to transgress but are equally unsure in themselves and anxious about doing so.

Trangression, therefore, is bound up with human ambivalence and the ambiguity of our world. It is also connected with action, cost and achievement—all characteristics of the atonement. Simply, therefore, to invoke the notion of reconciliation devalues the feelings of violence that need to be acknowledged in transgression. The pastor also needs to realize that in dealing with sin he is handling a state of mind which lies deep in feelings and often beyond words. Eventually such feelings may be articulated, but we need first to recognize that they are basically pre-verbal.

An illustration of this dimension to ministry is found in the initial stories of Jesus in Mark's Gospel. As soon as Jesus is fully into his role as healer and teacher, conflicts arise with the leaders of the prevailing culture as he heals a leper, plucks corn on the Sabbath, cures the man with a withered hand and is finally accused of being the devil's agent. Jesus boldly transgresses: by reinterpreting the bonds of convention which stifle people's freedom he effectively breaks them. But there is a second underlying theme. The stories also make the point that these controversies are mostly pre-verbal. The participants do not seem to engage with each other, and the arguments have a tangential quality which forebodes worse to come. We are, however, left in little doubt that both Jesus and his opponents feel strongly about the issues which are raised. Under the surface lies imminent violence. Indeed the textual tradition in Mark 1.41 demonstrates the edginess between profound feeling and anger. The word 'felt compassion' has as a weighty alternative 'was angry'. And anger is explicit in Mark 3.5. The strength of feeling is so strong that, at least at the start of his ministry, Jesus and those with whom he deals lack suitable categories or language through which to express themselves.

In this setting reconciliation is not the resolution of conflict or the recovery of a happier state of affairs. That would merely be to restore an existing constraint from which the person concerned is emerging with a struggle. There is a necessary anxiety about living which the pastor cannot and, on the basis of his theological insight through the window of the classic of the atonement, should not try to diminish. The cross and atonement as the model for his work affirms the fight/flight dynamic of human life and its characteristic of addressing ambivalence and producing anxiety. It is not Christian ministry, nor any form of reconciliation, to minimize this aspect of life. The atonement assigns central significance to feelings, and in so doing also affirms the importance of the fact that they are not easily articulated. This is the point of the pastor's involvement with sin or transgression, although the tradition of hearing confession and offering spoken counsel may obscure this. But this ministry, when rooted in a dynamic sense of transgression, both conforms to the theological model of the atonement and brings opportunity of salvation to individuals.

A useful concept to use in understanding this ministry is 'the holding environment'. Treatment of emotionally deprived people, often adolescents, may begin by constructing with them an environment which is designed to contain their feelings of anger and apathy, aggression and uninterest. Doctors, nurses and other workers do not provide this; it is negotiated in interaction with the patients as they respond to them in an assured, and therefore reassuring, fashion. Security that was hitherto absent is thus created and treatment can be provided [Shapiro 1982; Shapiro & Carr 1987].

The ministry of confession and absolution can be similarly viewed. The priest[1] and penitent, by meeting within particular constraints of time, place and formality, contract to create a temporary holding environment. In this the unsayable may be said and both have permission to articulate what is usually unspoken, even to oneself. But as the penitent speaks, he or she not only tells the priest of remembered sins and negligences; taking part in the process also involves reordering the penitent's internal world, just as negotiating the holding environment is part of the patient's treatment.

The priest, therefore, even in this most priestly of

ministries, is conforming to the pattern of ministry based upon the way of the cross. He is used — in the sense that the penitent makes what he or she will of him; this determines, for example, the form that the confession takes. The priest does not prescribe this, in spite of formularies. Indeed, the sensitive priest has to be prepared for things not to be what they seem: the penitent may talk in an allusive fashion; requests for advice may be expressions of immature, and inappropriate, dependence; self-assertion may be disguised as repentance.

The priest's counsel and, when required, judgement in response to the confession is interpretative. It may seem more directive than this, especially with the giving of penances. But interpretation is not giving answers; it is a function of the encounter itself, and so is a joint effort by the two concerned. Absolution, within this scheme, has a twofold function. In terms of transgression, it first clarifies the form that the sinner's transgressions have hitherto taken within the ambiguities of life and the ambivalence of our human nature. As a layperson recently commented in discussion: 'You clergy will not get anywhere with us until you realize that, while you talk about black and white, all our life is lived in grey.' Second, and paradoxically, absolution gives permission to transgress in the other sense of the term — to grow by risk. As we saw in thinking about the atonement, forgiveness is not the result of confession; it is the precondition. Although this is not necessarily the frame of mind with which the penitent comes, it is vital that it is the priest's framework of reference.

Pastoring and Projection

In everyday life projection is involved in the push for achievement. Those engaged in a struggle, for example, and eager to succeed in some course of action, are notoriously prone to misjudge reality. In their oversimplified world they rush towards their goal, real or imagined, headlong and careless of everything and everyone. By preventing us from seeing that what we are attacking is partly ourselves, projection can be a temporary way of alleviating stress, but only at cost to all concerned. The unconscious process brings relief to the person who is doing the projecting, and

simultaneously stirs up emotions in the recipient. The more
violent the projection, the more likely it is that the response
will be similarly marked. Caught in a cycle, people find
themselves becoming increasingly irrational.

But projection is not a ploy which we occasionally bring
out of our psychic cupboard. It is a basic ingredient in normal
human behaviour, and as such is a crucial constituent in
pastoral ministry. It is found in every relationship, and that
of the pastor with the penitent is not immune. Ministerial
expertise, therefore, is to follow this primary model of the
atonement and transform what is inhibiting or potentially
destructive to new creativity. When we realize that projection
constitutes basic human behaviour and is not a weakness or
failure, we can seek ways of employing it in the service of
pastoral ministry.

Ministry consists in being open to and available for the
projections of others by first ensuring that we can allow
ourselves to feel and perceive those projections for what they
are. The two primary questions, therefore, for ministers,
whatever the context, are always: 'What am I now being
made to feel?' and 'Why am I being made to feel this?' By first
examining the feelings we can begin to surmise about their
origins. There is no guarantee, of course, that we will answer
the questions correctly. But it is part of the skill of the
minister, his professionalism based on the model of the
crucified Christ, to acknowledge the significance of the feeling
dimension to human life and to try to discern which role he is
being assigned. In that way an appropriate response—or at
the least, a not too inappropriate one—may be offered. If we
are aware of the significance of all feelings, especially in the
projective world of relationships and expectations, we first
test why they seem to be found in us at this moment and in
this setting. Thus we have a good chance of beginning our
meeting with the person somewhere near the level of their
approach.

Projection and our natural tendency to use it defensively
can debilitate ministry. If, however, pastors can perceive it as
a pervasive facet of life, which God has specifically addressed
through the cross of Christ, then, in spite of being used,
abused and misused, they can find themselves doing
significant work with people. Projective behaviour and the

associated feelings, however, are not confined to the individual, as, for example, was the case with the confessional. These dynamics also underlie the activity of the local church as an identifiable part of a particular social context, as the following case study demonstrates.

Case Study

In a large village parish there were two church buildings with a congregation linked to each. One was the old church; the other a 'new' (nineteenth-century) building. The original reasons why the second church was built were complicated, but by the time of this story the village had largely developed around the newer church. It was in the centre of the largest segment of population, by the shops and adjacent to other amenities. The old church was on the fringe. The vicar was overstretched to provide a full range of services at both churches. In addition the village was not so large that the distances were too great to expect people who wished to worship to travel to the central church.

These were points of fact. But the vicar also believed that public expression of church unity was important as a statement of Christian belief and practice. He set out, therefore, on what he regarded as a ministry of reconciliation, not by closing one church but by fostering a stronger sense of unity in the whole parish and its expression in worship in one centre. He carefully involved the church council in consultation. Although different forms of worship prevailed in each church—the old services at the old church and newer ones at the central building—he was happy with this state of affairs, and indeed encouraged the council to think about how both forms of worship could continue to be provided.

He was experienced enough to expect disagreement. But he was unprepared for the irrational outburst that followed. Suddenly, and not only in the church, but throughout the village, unsuspected divisions emerged. Two camps were established on almost every issue that arose, not just the future of the church buildings. What is more, the members of each camp changed according to the issue. The vicar was bewildered. His previous experience failed him. He found irreconcilable splits developing in himself between, for instance, his intentions and actions and his gospel and his practice. He began to reckon that he was the wrong man for the parish and that he should, at cost to himself and his family, immediately move. The situation was suffused with anger, which was expressed at unexpected moments in strange ways. Friends became enemies; colleagues fell out over trivial matters. Irrational behaviour seemed uninterpretable. Sensible, competent people, among them the vicar, could not cope.

In various ways the vicar was made to feel that he was the cause of the problem. He first interpreted what was happening in terms of projections from all the parties directly into him. But after consultation a different perspective opened up. On examination it appeared that the hitherto uncontentious issue of two churches in a small village had long been used to contain many differences and arguments so that they remained unexpressed. Now, however, because the two churches themselves had been made the centre of attention, they could no longer function in this fashion in people's unconscious worlds. Consequently disarray prevailed and the vicar was a convenient focal point for people's ambivalences. He was a repository for the strong antipathies that different groups could not express to each other.

This behaviour was, in the terms that we are using, basic assumption activity. People found powerful but ambiguous feelings aroused in themselves. On the one hand they wished to get at each other and formed odd alliances to achieve this; on the other hand they longed to avoid any engagement. They were caught in fight/flight. All felt that they were struggling to achieve something important, but without any awareness that everybody's 'something' was insubstantial—their own needs. The vicar, who had inadvertently exposed these raw feelings, found that people displaced their anxieties and anger, together with their ambiguity and ambivalence, into the church leadership, namely him.

This is a simple instance of the corporate use of projection as a defence. Originally it had been against examining differences of self-awareness and intention in the church. This was conveniently provided by the existence of the two buildings. Each was being used by all concerned, not just by those who attended, to contain their uncertainties. In *both* congregations, for example, one group was concerned about the old services and another about the new. This struggle, familiar in any church, was in this case mainly avoided at the level of feeling by allowing one group to represent conservatism and the other innovation. Whether this was true or not remained unexamined. In fact each congregation included members with different views. It was easier, however, to project such ambivalence into the other congregation than to be responsible for a definite position within one's own.

When, having inadvertently removed this framework, the vicar began to promote the idea of reconciliation in the guise of a united fellowship of Christians, he, again unwittingly, created a nugatory focus for people's feelings. Christian fellowship, itself an ideal, was in this context nothing more than a fantasy. One reason was that the congregations were reflecting more than their internal dilemmas. There were also powerful divisions within the developing village community, in particular whether it was to hold on to its old image of itself or creatively to develop a new one. This idea of fellowship, therefore, sounded plausible, but proved insubstantial. Everyone's dilemma became worse. The ambivalence in the village as a whole was being projected into the different aspects of church life and contributing to its ambiguity; but these facets of church life themselves were being focused in something which all knew and felt to be unreal—idealized Christian fellowship.

The situation may appear irredeemable. But at this point, however, it became possible to act on the model of the atonement and to see how it could enable a Christian congregation to find God in these ambiguities and prevailing projections, and so deal with them realistically (in terms of its organization) and spiritually (in terms of its developing Christian life).

First, the vicar recognized that he had misinterpreted the situation, with hindsight almost inevitably. As leader of the church and as the focus of so much of the confusion, he had to surrender parts of himself, chiefly his ideal of a united church. This cleared the ground so that the projections that people were employing could be exposed. A further reality was also affirmed: there was no question in the vicar's mind of closing a church. This was in practice reinforced by the diocesan authorities, who, anticipating local developments, were not prepared to dispose of the building.

Second, a consistent stance was adopted. Every group, however important or apparently unimportant, was encouraged in its meetings to examine its internal divisions and was carefully dissuaded from the simple device of projecting them outwards. Thus they found themselves having to ask why such things mattered to them and so to take back what hitherto they had angrily disposed of into others. The question was always asked why it mattered both to them in their role or through them to the constituency that they represented. Here aspects of the way of the cross become explicit: representation and responsibility, as well as self-surrender in the interests of a greater task. They were not made to feel guilty for having used others. There would have been no future in that; any such sense was a spin-off, not a central concern. They were, however, deliberately asked to examine their own feelings and beliefs.

Third, the exercise was set in a wider context than that which people usually employed. In the cross the political and social factors which coincided are important but not in the end central. Jesus' death tests everything, and to do that has to be specifically set among questions about the nature of God himself. In this case, if discussion had been by church people in the context of church life alone, it might be instructive but probably not effective. The notion of a whole church, which had been used, had proved an illusion. So church people were invited to try and think about what was happening to them in the setting of the village community as a whole, of which they were also members. It soon became apparent that the congregations were colluding with the village as a whole in ignoring one area. The village included a housing estate, which was unconnected with either church or with either end of the village. It was marginal in every way. The village community and the church seemed to be dividing over comparatively unimportant issues so as not to have to address a major reality about the village—how this housing estate was to be incorporated into its life.

This process involved heavy cost. The vicar had to abandon ideas which were very dear to him. The congregations and groups within them had to undergo the pain of repentance and change. The effort of thinking in the way described also carried a cost. Inevitably, therefore, a few individuals could not endure and left. But by now most members of the congregation and the vicar were sufficiently sensitized to projection that they were able, so far as they could, to avoid allowing these few to carry off unresolved feelings of anger and disarray. This work was evidenced by the fact that to everyone's surprise so small a number left. The tensions of ministry in the village remain, and the divisions are not magically healed or reconciled. But the change now is that because they can be acknowledged they can be explored, interpreted and used. The basic dynamic remains; but it is now harnessed to a task of ministry rather than given expression through the idealized notion of fellowship.

This case is particularly useful for thinking about ministry in the light of those aspects of our behaviour which God has explicitly addressed through the cross. We tend to consider how individuals affect each other through forgiveness and reconciliation. These issues have to do with the cross and atonement. But the death of the one individual, Jesus of Nazareth, is nothing unless it is interpreted in its setting within the major political and social movements of the time — and unless the whole complex event is put in the context of God's total activity with the world. When, therefore, we consider pastoral practice in the light of this classic, it is valuable to be reminded that it is also directed to structural issues of organization.

The role of the pastor is, as we have noted, a function of the task of the church in its context. When people approach a minister for care, absolution or advice, whatever their stated wish, they are approaching a publicly religious figure and so addressing something which that role represents to them, whether they consciously realize this or not. The minister may experience this as affirming or denying. We receive a variety of projections, usually at the same time. They therefore need disentangling. The key to this unravelling lies in focusing on feelings that are confusingly aroused in us. We should not expect them to be otherwise. People bring with them ideas about God and religion which are not likely to be sophisticated and articulate but primitive and incapable of being spoken.

Nevertheless the model of the atonement undergirds and

emphasizes how important is this phase of pastoral ministry. Through the cross God himself accepts and interprets the fantasies that are projected on to him, specifically the dependent fantasy that magic can in the end be expected. What does it mean for men and women and God himself that the offered saviour does not perform the ultimate miracle?

> There [i.e. on the cross] above all and for the last time the miracle did not take place. 'Let the Christ, the King of Israel, come down now from the cross, that we may see and believe' (Mark 15.32), they shout. And they kept on shouting while he perished in misery. And the miracle, boldly demanded, secretly expected, devoutly hoped for, ardently prayed for, did not take place. [Schweizer 1971, 45]

This is the issue, however, with which in the gospel stories Jesus himself first has to struggle. He has to live with and acknowledge his own feelings, which are profoundly affected by the contradictory projections of his disciples and the crowd, in order to be able to interpret these back to them. The cost of that interpretation in this case was the crucifixion. But because he offers back interpreted projections at this ultimate cost to himself, others are eventually able to struggle with the nature of their own belief.

The cross is the basis of pastoral ministry in the context of projection. First, we realize that such projections, although they stir up powerful feelings, are chiefly directed to the minister's roles. Second, we discover that opportunities for interpretative ministry arise as we accept these roles and the associated projections and, exploring the feelings generated in us, use them as the basis for our response to people. Thus the Christian story becomes gospel — good news. It is generated as we respond to people's assumptions about us as God's representatives with our life and corresponding interpretative stance informed by Scripture, tradition and faith. Third, this position holds us, in the face of pressure to adopt other stances that are sometimes more congruent with the assumptions of the age or with our own self-image, to our priestly role as the significant point of address.[2] In so doing we shall not confuse, for example, penitents by treating them as clients or normal souls seeking ministry by treating them as neurotic.

Guilt and Forgiveness

As a presumed man of God, the pastor will inevitably be invited to deal with guilt and forgiveness. Indeed these are probably lurking somewhere on the agenda of most people who approach him. This is a dangerous area, where clarity is important. Guilt may be a form of fear and anxiety which, through a personality disorder, becomes morbid. The Church has sometimes made a speciality of this, inducing it in order to absolve it. But there is also a proper sense of guilt, of which the penitent can be aware and so forgiven. This sort of guilt, which is self-engendered, is less widely recognized today, since the notion of guilt as a form of disorder tends to dominate popular thought. The pastor needs to understand that guilt is not necessarily a condition but a set of feelings arising from the basic ambiguity and ambivalence of the human condition. Guilt, therefore, is also endemic and cannot be casually removed or explained. But these two facets — the morbid and the proper — are also intertwined. When dealing with someone feeling guilty we are touching primitive parts of their deepest self. Such guilt, therefore, will not be lightly removed by absolution nor can it be ritually abolished. The pastor first needs discernment.

Guilt arises from feelings of being crushed in our interactions. These are with other people, with our own inner worlds or more generally with the context in which we live. This is why guilty feelings are difficult to locate. The experience is of being caught both ways. For example, over the centuries Christians have been confused on the issue of slavery, which now seems clear. Here all three interactions, with others, with ourselves and with our context, come together. The earliest Christians seem to have been unaware that slavery might be an evil. They displayed little, if any, guilt for what was done to fellow human beings and were devoid of feelings. As, however, awareness grew, people began to feel guilty and many, finally most, shifted from their indifference as these feelings were interpreted, the complexity of their guilt was eventually perceived and absolution followed action — the freeing of slaves.

But guilt has a double edge: on the one hand we feel guilt for our ignorance in not noticing that anything is wrong; on the other hand there is also guilt for our knowledge, when that comes about. We are crushed in a pincer movement between ignorance and knowledge and between ourselves and our external world, from which there seems no escape. We participate in a world that we do not necessarily enjoy but which also orders our ways of participating. Forgiveness, therefore, would not be release from that guilt, since it would become release from the world. Flight of this kind is uncreative and leads to religion becoming that delusion which has been so accurately diagnosed in this century. The first stage to forgiveness is to allow people their ambivalence and to acknowledge it. This sounds dully conformist, but it is, as the cross shows, the first step towards salvation: 'It is all this that Christian traditions invite us to celebrate in the sacrament of forgiveness: tensions, conflicts, transgressions, prophetic words or actions, the confession of new sins, the request for forgiveness, and the acceptance of forgiveness accorded' [Fourez 1983, 108].

Such guilt is a basic human condition which needs to be affirmed as the first step to forgiveness, absolution and the recovering of responsibility. The minister bases this affirmation on his grasp of the cross of Christ. He can then go further. Forgiveness does not free us from the guilt which is a dimension of our humanity; it is transformed from being destructive to creative. The popular belief that to forgive is to forget is seriously at fault when we recognize that men and women are responsible beings with conscious and unconscious worlds. Where deep feelings, whatever their origin, are concerned, forgetfulness is impossible. They and their origins may be consciously forgotten, but they remain in our unconscious mind and may later emerge, much to everyone's surprise. The secret of forgiveness is remembrance, to rehearse the past so as to acknowledge it as ours.

The Christian proclamation of forgiveness through the cross of Christ makes precisely this point. The historical moment of crucifixion becomes the turning-point in Christian teaching. Remembrance becomes a way of living. Whatever else may be lost, dismissed or fantasized away, there is no gospel without recourse to at least one historical reality—a crucifixion. Even when this remembrance is ritualized in worship, it still refers to a specific moment. The eucharistic canon itself holds the cross at the centre of the Church's worship, where the worshippers 'show forth the Lord's death' (1 Cor. 11.26). And from earliest times the creeds included the phrase 'under Pontius Pilate' to root salvation in history. So Rufinus in the fourth century remarks: 'Those who handed down the creed showed great wisdom in underlining the actual date at which these things happened, so that there might be no chance of any uncertainty or vagueness upsetting the stability of the tradition' [Kelly 1972, 151].

A vital ingredient in any ministry modelled on the atonement is a similar emphasis on detail. It reminds the minister that all interpretation, even of the vast issues of human life and meaning, has to be focused, not just in a general sense to the person concerned but also specifically through the minister's actual feelings in that particular encounter. He is consistently pulled back from the world of fantasies to what is here and now, what can be recalled.

Undergirding the pastoral response to guilt and forgiveness are two further facets of the atonement. The first is the familiar one of unconditional acceptance and grace. Here a grasp of morbid and proper guilt is essential. A major problem with people who feel acute guilt is that they cannot accept themselves. It is no use speaking to them of the accepting grace of God, since they have insufficient sense of their self to which to apply it. The pastor needs the *model* of the atonement to work with rather than any easy assumption about its benefits. His role is to embody this acceptance by willingly receiving projections on behalf of God before attempting to offer them back in interpretation. Held thus, those with guilty souls are given space and assurance to discover to what extent they might become able to accept themselves.

In this consideration of guilt and the pastor's dealing with it we are in a larger field than that of formal confession and absolution. We have previously seen how that occupies a negotiated setting, in which there are reasonably defined roles: priest, with authority to hear confession and offer absolution, and penitent, in the role of one seeking formal forgiveness. These public roles may obscure several others which are covertly assumed, but they are the basis of the encounter. Here, however, we are considering the over-whelming, generalized role that the minister may possess by virtue of being regarded as 'the God-person'. Pastors are thus foci for a range of projections, and taking these is a thankless task. But the pastor is sustained by the cross, where God demonstrates that it is his way of working to hold projections and sustain them against every pressure to discount or dismiss them. Even when, therefore, projection from a penitent on to him as a representation of God becomes acute, the minister knows that he is not being asked to be something other than he is or to handle the impossible. He has his given model as the basic notion by which to sustain his ministry.

Second, in the Christian tradition forgiveness is confirmed by action. Forgiveness is not a feeling or a state but an experience that is demonstrated in action. By this means the orientation towards achievement, which is the mark of the fight/flight dynamic that underlies crucifixion and atonement, is preserved. The action chiefly possesses symbolic signifi-cance, since it will always be inadequate. But it reminds the penitent, the minister and others that reconciliation is neither easy nor ever complete. Because it always includes potential change, it has a forward look to it and must remain open to new possibilities.

The cross of Christ is concerned with achievement and hopeful possibilities of change and newness. Forgiveness of the past implies future action based upon that past. That is why any notion of eradicating that past is theologically, pastorally and psychologically false. Forgiveness is not losing what has been acquired, however debased it may on reflection seem, and even if it is a cause for guilt. Whatever guilt may desire, absolution recovers and revalues some formative experiences or behaviour, which will not and cannot be lost. They remain, but they no longer need crush.

Evangelism and the Cross

Today's Churches and ministers are worried about the Churches' evangelistic task. The classic of the atonement is the heart of the gospel proclamation. St Paul defines it: 'We preach Christ and him crucified' (1 Cor. 1.23). The evangelist, like the pastor, is called to embody Christ, so that through him people may uncover some of their profound projections. The proclamation, therefore, is of Christ's cross as the way which all are invited to follow. It is not composed of assured consequences which some may have derived for themselves from meditation upon that way. When, therefore, we take up pastoral ministry on the basis of the cross, we become increasingly sensitive to what the gospel is and how it can be explicitly proclaimed.

This is a proper feeling in the light of our present discussion, since evangelism is a mobilizing of the dynamic of fight. It is essentially an aggressive stance, emphasizing that the proclaimer has a message to impart to others. In this sense, therefore, it is similar to marketing in its demand for behaviour which is orientated towards achievement. Yet, as we have seen, this dynamic is the one most prone to supporting fantasies and delusion about oneself, about others and about the message. To be effective, a fight has to be at the right time, in the right place, and about the right issue.

This way of the cross is marked by that integrity which persistently faces reality and lives with it. It speaks of affirmed ambivalence and ambiguity; of the cost of achievement; of the demands of personal integrity; and of effective living on behalf of others. These are the evangelistic themes which are illuminated by the powerful story of the crucifixion. To be saving they have specifically to address the person hearing rather than express a particular doctrine. Most forms of evangelism have at some time been criticized as indulging in projection. But this accusation is no reason for special anxiety. All human interactions, as we have seen, are to some extent projective. The test of the evangelist, which itself derives from the cross he proclaims, is what is done with those projections, both those that he receives and, more importantly, his upon the hearers. The clue to this, and to evangelism today, lies in the notion of the witness.

The Christian witness does not say his piece on every occasion; he embodies what he proclaims even to death, if needs be, as martyr.[3] Evangelism, therefore, is not just preaching, with the attendant risk of the evangelist merely projecting into his audience. It must include somewhere in its process the struggle to interpret projections, received and given. Like Christ, a person who claims to speak the word of God should expect to deal with projections which people believe that they cannot effectively direct to God himself. They are thrown at God through the evangelist, and so become for him both primary data about the people he is addressing and simultaneously data for creating God's word in that context. It seems unlikely, therefore, that evangelism can take place according to the model of the cross without personal engagement, or, at least, a context which fosters that sense in those being addressed. This may be a question that needs further thought in our world of media and new forms of communication, in so far as they may implicitly encourage the belief that personal engagement may be less important than the mere presentation of the message [Morris 1984].

The supposed conflict between pastoring and evangelizing, which is sometimes argued among the Church's ministers, is another instance of that defensive splitting and projection that marks our human lives, and it too stands under the judgement of the cross. Aggressive connotations to the gospel, however, do need to be recognized, not just in terms of how the Christian addresses his own feelings of anger and rage, but also when we ask how they can be mobilized to create activity on the part of the people of God. We are, therefore, now at the point to consider which aspect of our religious life is addressed by the classic of the atonement.

Notes

1 The word 'priest' is deliberately used here, because formally confession and absolution have been part of the priest's function. However, readers who do not hold this view of ministry will be able to substitute their own description of this minister and whatever setting would for them replace the confessional.

2 The word 'priestly' is again deliberately used here, but not to refer to technical issues of ordained priesthood. It describes the priestly stance that is required of every Christian minister [Carr 1985a].

3 The first unequivocal use of the word 'martyr' to designate one who witnesses and dies is in connection with Polycarp, who died in Smyrna in 155 CE (*Martyrdom of Polycarp* 19.1), but the link between witness and death goes back to Stephen (Acts 22.20), and (implicitly) to Jesus' crucifixion (Rev. 1.5).

TEN

Atonement and the Disciples' Spirituality

The way of discipleship is spirituality. The word is, however, over-used. Churches hold working parties and recruit committees, organize discussion groups and train spiritual directors in order to discover its content. Some problems with the idea arise because the word changes its meaning at different moments in the Church's history. So when we are pointed to the so-called 'spiritual classics', we usually find that the writers are not quite dealing with our questions. The term oscillates between the private concern and preoccupation with religious activity and a way of viewing and informing the whole of life. 'Spiritual', for example, has referred to the professional religious life of the clergy, along with the possessions of the Church. Alternatively it can define matters which contrast with material concerns. The spiritual life is always in danger of being restricted to higher or, so it is believed, more important areas than those in which most human beings live. But at its best, spirituality concerns the meaning of everyday life. It speaks of a life informed by and responding to belief in God. The term describes the profound quality of ordinary human life, and because of that it presses a fundamental ambivalence on those who would be spiritual. They constantly have to ask whether they find themselves in a particular situation because they are human beings or because they are Christian disciples.

This is a false antithesis, but one that none the less emerges in confessions and discussions. However unreal in theory, it is an experience which is felt in practice. It, therefore, cannot be removed by theological rationale but has to be faced as a phenomenon of human and religious life. For example, God must ultimately be and remain unknowable. This belief, however, does not derive solely from the problems of knowing

155

God—his essential hiddenness. It is part of our ambivalence in the face of those factors which, like God, enlarge the dimensions within which we live. We want them but fear them. In the tradition of the dark night of the soul, for example, we discover a sense of the hidden God at the same time as we are faced with our blinded soul's unwillingness to see his light. It is neither one nor the other, but both.

Christian discipleship or spirituality is marked by the same characteristics as the Christian classic of the cross: ambivalence in ourselves; ambiguity in our context; the need for decision and action; and the question of cost. These are also, as we have noted, marks of common human experience. Although, therefore, some debased forms of discipleship may seem to be superimposed on everyday life, there is no future in this approach for the Christian way of life. Christian spirituality is the human journey lived in the illumination and under the judgement of the way of the cross. It is, therefore, a way of discomfort, not because of any morbid wish pathologically to identify ourselves with the suffering Christ, but because it affirms the ambivalence and ambiguity in our human condition.

Spirituality and Ambivalence

We have seen how ambivalence is an achieved state in our development, built upon the profound anxiety of our earliest life. Ambivalence, therefore, itself is ambivalent: it is an achievement, but one which is always questioned. It persists in the form of doubt. The dependence which characterizes religious belief makes doubt appear as a reprehensible form of unfaithfulness. But within the dynamic of fight/flight doubt is essential. If we are not uncertain about ourselves, our decisions, our world, or our meaning, then we are not open to the options available to us. We have implicitly closed some down. Doubt is valued ambivalence, which gives us a chance to be creative, because it alerts us to the potential for change when we engage both our inner world and our context.

This human feeling represents everyone's potential as a child of God. The complexities of life are such that we sometimes feel that to survive we need to become more sure about ourselves and our place within the world. But feeling doubtful about this, we excuse ourselves and propel ourselves into guilt. This type of guilt, however, as we noted, is appropriate to human beings; it can be forgiven by confirming that the ambivalent feelings, which have generated it, are desirable because they arise from what we all are—creatures in God's creation.

The central Christian teaching on this, which is embodied in the death of Jesus, is that the way of discipleship is that of forgiveness, particularly of those whom we perceive as enemies. This goes to the heart of changing oneself and changing the world, because it simultaneously brings about three effects, each of which offers hope.

First, we take back the negative aspects of ourselves which contribute to our definition of 'enemy'. The stronger the feeling of hostility towards someone, however justified, the more it includes aspects of ourselves. Change here first requires honesty. Facing this and so taking back as best we may our projections, we are changed. Second, by doing this we actually affect the 'enemy'. As negative projection is recognized and withdrawn, his feelings are also altered. Whatever the causes of his hostility—and this does not pretend to be a total explanation—he will at least be freed from responding to projections from us which he probably does not understand but which he certainly feels. The free, or forgiven, person brings hope to others. Third, the relationship itself is adjusted. We are not, therefore, in speaking of forgiveness merely outlining an approach to person-to-person relationships. We are also talking about a fundamental change in the structures within which they are locked and the interrelation between them, a discernible shift in an otherwise blocked world. The way of discipleship is to embody affirmed, redeemed and so creative ambivalence.

Spirituality and Ambiguity

The ambivalence within us is matched by the ambiguity of our context. We know that we are bound up in a network of relationships and institutions, some of which we dimly perceive and most of which lie beyond our comprehension. Every specific context, when given our attention, becomes

ambiguous. When we think we may have sorted ourselves
out, the world confuses us. The core of Christian spirituality,
however, is not a private affair of survival within the chaos; it
is concerned with social involvement — that is, being part of
the human race and the created order.

It is important, however, that we acknowledge how
inherently ambiguous all human life is. One consequence of
failing to grasp this may be seen in a contemporary issue of
discipleship — the disagreements between Christian Churches,
which seem increasingly inappropriate in today's world.
Ecumenical striving is an attempt to remove such discord.
But the hope is misplaced. Dissension is not solely grounded
in church structures and ancient or modern disputes. These
contribute, but largely as vehicles for our difficulties in dealing
with our human context. As units in their social setting
churches participate as much as any other bodies in the
prevailing confusions of the world. But they incorporate these
into a confined space of belief or religious practice. There, so
it is believed, profound dissension can be effectively understood. But by thinking in terms of 'understanding', Christians
casually translate contemporary difficulty into historical
terms. They then produce the customary ecumenical document:
a worthy statement of intent, a long historical excursus, and
usually brief proposals for action. Since the latter, however,
chiefly derive from the historical excursus rather than from
the realities of present-day experiences of disciples, they are
difficult to implement. In this way, however, we convince
ourselves that we can avoid the problems of living with the
ambiguity of religious belief, which finds expression in the
different churches, and with the various social dynamics,
which lead to distinctive expectations being focused in these
separate churches by the communities in which they are set.
We pretend that the problems of living merely originate from
profound doctrinal differences.

These are genuine concerns for Christian discipleship and
spiritual growth. Yet we need to recognize that the underlying
factor is the ambiguity of our context, because this, too, the
cross endorses as more than an unfortunate problem. Every
setting in which something has to be done includes
possibilities of success and failure. The cross itself is a
specific paradigm of this at one point in history. This

ambiguity and uncertainty mobilizes fight/flight, the very dynamic which, as we saw earlier, is stimulated from our earliest moments by our increasingly coming to terms with our outside world. In other words, the ambiguity of the world is not something to be endured; it is to be accepted and enjoyed as what enables us to exist at all. Under stress we may curse the world and blame God for allowing it to be as it is. From this dilemma, however, as Job discovered, spiritual maturity will not allow us so comfortable an escape. His story is confirmed in the Christian spiritual tradition based on the way of the cross, a way of engagement, risk, error and forgiveness.

Spirituality and Action

When we have taken into account ambivalence and ambiguity, there remains the need to do something. If deciding is problematic, acting is more so. Yet action is intrinsic to Christian spirituality. There are no passive individuals or groups either on or around the cross. Each has a decision to make and an action consequent upon it. Similarly with the Christian way: action is necessary, and decisions without action are void. That is why mission and evangelism are bound up with Christian spirituality, and without them spirituality is a debased concept.

To emphasize the significance of action for spirituality is not to conform to the ideas of success which prevail in our frenetic world. This dismal form of spiritual teaching is sometimes proclaimed in the name of Christ. Yet it is not based on the realities of the atonement but on collusion between the teacher and the audience's dependent longings which render them gullible. When this happens religion again proves a delusion. Yet action, as a basic ingredient of the pattern of the cross, provides the critical norm for Christian decision-making and action. Disciples act in such a fashion as to become available and vulnerable to the scrutiny of others. Like Christ, they become a window through which people can gain a glimpse of a depth in their being, which is God. Or, we might say more traditionally, they become Christ to their neighbour.

Luther's bold exhortation in his letter to Melancthon in

1556, 'Be a sinner and sin strongly, but more strongly have faith and rejoice in Christ,' captures this vision [Luther 1556, i.345]. Although he was speaking of divine grace, the remark implies that this exercise also tests God himself. Similarly the Christian is continually exhorted to act decisively, not in order to test God but to become accessible to others for their scrutiny. Without the risk of action Christians cease to be identifiable, the gospel becomes shrouded, and spiritual life will become introverted as mission declines.

There are today, as ever, deep divisions over what constitutes Christian action. Social and political activity is so rife in society that a distinctive Christian contribution is difficult to determine. The cross, however, provides some indicators for the activity of discipleship. First, because it is set in a historical context and represents not only actions between God and his world but between God and himself, it suggests that action based on this model is collaborative. This word has recently been applied to shared activity between laity and ordained ministers in the phrase 'collaborative ministry'. The disciples' spirituality based on the classic of the atonement will not be particularly distinguished by this. It will, however, be marked by the only collaboration that matters—that between Christians and others—because in this meeting Christ himself is found.

Second, the hazard of the cross reminds Christians that, contrary to their deep-felt instincts derived from a sense of thankfulness and awe, God does not need their protection. Any action is risky, especially if it involves someone else's name, not least God's. But the model of the way of the cross provides a critical test of action. The question is not only 'Is it shared?', but also 'Has it been and will it continue to be scrutinized?' and 'Will our activity encourage this stance in others, whatever their belief?'

What Christians do, therefore, is important, although it may be exactly what others are also doing. The distinctive mark of Christian spirituality is the way in which these actions are consciously used to allow, and encourage, scrutiny by others and the vulnerability that follows. Here we come to the final issue—that of cost.

Spirituality and Cost

When we act on behalf of others and are used by them, wittingly and unwittingly, cost becomes important. There are bound to be mistakes and hurts with their consequent feelings. And when feelings are rife, blame—apportionment of cost—erupts. Blame and recrimination follow error. Such costs can be absorbed, often without too much difficulty, because when something goes wrong it does not always require much virtue from people to accept that they were involved. There is nothing specially Christian about this or about the fights that are sometimes engendered. On the question of such everyday costs Christians are called to be an example. They pale into insignificance for disciples of the crucified. In other words, by accepting blame that may not directly belong to them, they can extend an invitation to others to live responsibly in a similar fashion. This is part of the way of the cross—'When he was reviled, he reviled not again' (1 Pet. 2.23). This aspect of that cross directly connects with common human experience, and anyone, believer or not, can be invited to live responsibly in this fashion.

There is, however, a further type of cost, which is harder to accept. It is a central mark of Christian spirituality enlivened by the cross of Christ. To accept and absorb blame for things for which we are not responsible is a dangerous enterprise. It can lead to patronizing others, the pathology of omnipotence and that eagerness to placate everyone which sometimes marks so-called 'Christian' behaviour. Yet bearing costs on behalf of others is Christlike and lies deep in the disciple's spirituality. As with God's work in Christ, the aim is not to relieve others of their responsibilities. The delicate task is to hold responsibility for what does not belong to us so that others may be able to resume or discover their responsibility within God's world. Such self-critical bearing of blame and pain for others is not a permanent state. The skill of the disciple in such ministry is to take up the priestlike task, which is to stand for someone else at a point in their life where, for whatever reason, for the time being they cannot stand [Carr 1985a]. This life on behalf of others is both the stance of Christ and the essence of Christian spirituality.

'On behalf of' is the ultimate clue to the Christian

interpretation of life and understanding of God. It, therefore, also informs Christian spirituality and is the point at which the fact of the cross of Christ tests discipleship so that it does not become debased. The New Testament writers usually use the preposition *huper* for this attitude, and, less frequently, *anti*. *Huper* can follow words which cover almost every aspect of discipleship: prayer, working and caring, sacrifice, suffering and dying, and generally being. All the Christian classics and the activities rooted in them are in the end tested by the extent that they are testably believed and lived on behalf of others. In the cross, however, we encounter the complete manifestation of this way. God himself demonstrates life devoid of self-interest and wholly lived on behalf of others.

Spirituality and Sacraments

Spirituality is sometimes thought of as worship and prayer. But these alone do not involve and convert others. When separated from the critical testing of life, which is the way of discipleship, they become maudlin and self-centred. They lose contact with the awesome reality of a God who works through both the starkness of the cross and the confusions of everyday human existence and are used as escape routes for people in flight. For a while they may be speciously justified as profound trust in God or an intimate relationship with him. But eventually they fail, unless we realize that every experience of faith is enjoyed only vicariously.

This sense of 'on behalf of' is sustained by the classic of the cross and by the life lived upon affirmed ambivalence and ambiguity, decisive (even if sometimes mistaken) action, and responsible bearing of cost on behalf of others in the interests of their taking a step further towards their responsibility as human beings. Such is the complex, double dynamic of fight/flight, in which we find robustly functional faith, which brings about change in individuals and in the world — salvation.

There is an interchange between the centre of the Christian faith and human life, which allows Christians to commend the way of the cross as an interpretative tool for living, without first requiring that people believe the Christian message. This stance is confirmed by and permanently enshrined in the two dominical sacraments, each of which is notably a sacrament of the cross—baptism and Eucharist. But each of these central components of Christian faith and spirituality uses natural symbols. Even when Christians attempt to retain them as the prerogative of the believing community—an entry rite and a fellowship meal—they do not lose their wide range of associations. They break out of these confines as people use them. By their nature water, bread and wine can never become private property of the Christian Church [Carr 1985b]. Thus what Christians most intimately cling to as the focus of their corporate spirituality of the cross turns out to be the property of mankind. Thus again the particularity of the Christian profession and its universal implication unite.

The cross, Christian spirituality and sacramental thinking coalesce to display divine grace. The Christian gospel finally stands by this statement: You do not have to be a believer to approach God, whether through word or sacrament. Believers, therefore, far from possessing a message from God that they have at all costs to convey to their fellow men and women, are those marked by vulnerability to the scrutiny of their fellow human beings. The Church has been instinctively right to resist promulgating one orthodox doctrine of the atonement. The power of the cross and the strength of those who walk its way lie in vulnerability, whether to historical investigation or to scrutiny in the lives of those who profess a Christian spirituality.

C. Permissible Madness: The Classic of the Creation and Resurrection

In respect to these transitional objects the parents, as it were, conspire not to challenge the origins. They easily see that the thumb is part of the child and that the next toy or teddy bear or doll is a gift, but with regard to the object in question they undertake to refrain from challenging the infant as to its origin. There is madness here which is permissible . . . The madness is that this object is created by the infant and also it was there in the environment for the infant's use.

(D. W. Winnicott [*S. Deri 1978, 56*])

ELEVEN

The Classic of Creation

The third Christian classic is the most complex. It incorporates both the classic of creation and the classic of resurrection. Therefore in this section, unlike the preceding two, there are two chapters of theological reflection before we turn to pastoral practice and discipleship. The dynamic which underlies both creation and resurrection—dependence—permeates human life and is specially prominent when we think of the Church and its gospel [Reed 1978; Carr 1985a]. From whichever angle we approach this doctrine—theological, pastoral, in terms of discipleship or from the psychodynamic perspective—it looks massive. The nature of God and the fact of religion join in demanding congruent theological understanding. It is also the most immediate classic. Ministers daily deal with this area of human and religious experience. Any better understanding of it, therefore, should illuminate every aspect of church life and ministry, as well as the content of the gospel to be proclaimed.

When asked by a visiting consultant what her connection with the local church was, one lady rapidly distanced herself from it. She did not believe in God or religion; the church authorities were soulless, careless of the beautiful building of which they were custodians; the vicar was at best irrelevant to the life of the town and at worst a malign influence. But when it was suggested that logically the church building should be closed and the vicar deployed more usefully elsewhere, she immediately and instinctively responded, 'Oh no! We are our past, and the church is the only guardian of that past. It is a comfort to know that the vicar prays for the town and the world' [Carr 1985a, 6].

Most ministers are familiar with this sort of response. Beyond the congregation there is a penumbra of those who claim membership of the Church and who from time to time seem to need to express some form of belief—the people of folk, common, or implicit religion. A major crisis in national or personal life—a war, the birth of a child, a relative's death—may stir unsuspected feelings. These generate anxiety, which is expressed in a wish to be near the source of power, perhaps God or the priest or the Church, but not to get too involved with it. This often frustrates clergy and ministers. As public religious figures they are used by people to represent the nearness and distance of a desired but also undesirable god, with whom but also without whom people prefer to live. And in the West such a god inevitably has Christian hues.

Any integration of theology and pastoral practice must take account of folk religion. This sense of awe and superstition is the material with which ministers and churches work. Attempts to isolate 'true faith' from 'religion' are doomed. The phenomenon of religion is inextricably bound up with faith, and will neither go away nor purify itself of its folk accretions and manifestations. Faith, religion and the insistent demand for ritual coincide in worship. This cannot be confined, as sometimes in the contemporary Church, to liturgy. We are in a wider field of belief about some being, usually called 'God', who is reckoned to impinge upon us and to whom a response should be made.

With this classic we have first to deal with the basic condition of all of life—creation. Then we discuss the distinctively Christian vision of the new creation, the resurrection.

Potential and Limitation

Behind 'We believe in God . . . creator of heaven and earth' lie three affirmations. First, the world, of which we are part and to which we contribute, is what there is and invites interpretation. Because we exist and think objectively and imaginatively about the world, we contribute to its creation. But we do not completely create it. From a psychological perspective people may be said to create their worlds. But for this to happen there must be people to do the creating. There are, therefore, given factors, which we sometimes feel as constraints and which condition what is possible. Theological responses to this observation vary. But there is no escape from the obvious: there is what there is, however much of this giveness is at any moment undiscovered or unexplored. And this world, the one which we know and not some other, demands some attempt at interpretation.

The second affirmation is that God comes first. 'God is creator' announces God's freedom, since of his own free will he began it all. It might seem, however, that the modern insight that we create in our own worlds contradicts this affirmation. If we remain locked into a simplistic view, this could be the case. But the ability to create our own worlds is a function of our imagination. In contemporary thought such creativity is being increasingly acknowledged as having a central place: in psychoanalysis [Winnicott 1971; Rycroft 1985]; in mathematics and philosophy [Polanyi 1958]; in theology [Kaufmann 1981] and in religious studies [Bowker 1973; Bowker 1978]. Through imagination we respond to something that is not immediately present in our environment but which we feel is potentially there. We use it to create ideas and imagined worlds. But when we describe this activity we use the language of receiving. Ideas 'strike us', 'come to us', 'occur' and so on. Imaginative activity is a facet of our experience which is a goal to which we strive but which also appears to come from beyond us. When, therefore, we become aware of our own creative activity, we do not necessarily dispute God's priority.

Thirdly we affirm that God's creation is out of nothing (*ex nihilo*). 'Out of "the inner necessity of his love", to use Barth's phrase, the Creator makes something that corresponds to him and gives him pleasure' [Moltmann 1979, 120]. We creatures are finite and mortal because we depend on God for our continued existence. If creation originates in God alone, we can regard the process as purposeful. This purpose is the object of our search for our own creatureliness, leading us to study what there is and who we are. But such belief also implies that God may generate new possibilities and that creation is not limited to what at present is—although that is all that may remain accessible to us—but includes what might be. The danger of such an argument is that unbounded speculation may be let loose. Some controls or norms are, therefore, needed as criteria by which to judge. In our Judaeo-Christian tradition we find these, as we shall later see, by reflection on the new creation, which for Christians becomes specifically the resurrection.

Each of these three fundamental issues highlights the tension between potential and limitation. Creation resounds with the potential of unlimited possibilities, but there are in fact limits to what there is and what is accessible to us. The priority of God emphasizes the potential of his freedom to do whatever he wishes, but contrasts it with the limitation implied by his stance of love. And the gap between what we finite human beings can imagine, our unbounded vision, and what we achieve points in the same direction of potential and limitation.

St Augustine provides a notable account of the personal disarray that may ensue when we grasp this tension of potential and limitation within ourselves and our world. He wished to have nothing to do with God, but found that God remained faithful to him and that flight was finally impossible and confessed: 'You have made us for yourself and our heart is restless until it finds its rest in you' (*Confessions* 1.1). The remark is not distinctively Christian. It captures the general sense of dependent longing for security in the face of life's ambiguities. It might imply that Augustine wished to surrender his autonomy by giving up responsibility for his behaviour and settling for quietism. Some, both within the Christian community and outside, argue that this is precisely the nature of Christian faith and commend Augustine's frankness. But there is another possibility. Augustine makes his dependence conscious and is thus able to resume his responsibilities as a human being. He is describing the basic human dilemma between surrendering and acknowledging responsibility.

The more we become aware that we are autonomous beings, the more we simultaneously discover the frustrations which are imposed from inside and outside ourselves. So the more sensitive and alert we are to our human autonomy and the more eager we become to act on the responsibilities that go with it, the more we realize that the only way to its exercise is by surrendering parts of it. To develop potential we have to come to terms with limitations. Caught in this lived dilemma, we are bound from time to time to regress to our primary condition of dependence.[1] But we may view such regression either as a weakness or as a description of a process which is a necessary part of the reality of ourselves and our worlds. This complex of the world as it is, our dependent life within it, and our contribution to it, is the foundation of the classic of the creation.

Creation and Dependence in Human Experience

Dependence and creation go hand in hand. Our lives begin merged with our mother and relying upon her (or, after birth, some other). Psychological 'birth' does not take place at the same time as physical birth, but begins as we go through the processes of becoming individuals. However, the sense of reliance on another persists, and throughout our adult life, however mature we may become, at various moments we revert to it [Mahler et al. 1975]. Dependence, therefore, is not opposed to individuality or autonomy. All three are complementary aspects of those processes which create and sustain us as people and which manifest themselves both in individual and in group behaviour. They are integral to our being as creatures. But creatures are not complete in themselves, unchanging or immortal. Creatureliness is perennially reasserted through three experiences which are common to us all: death and decay; the sense of history, or time passing; and our awareness that experience itself is fragmented. But as a way into exploration of God, our creaturely dependence looks promising.

a) Decay, death and dependence

Decay and death, both personal ageing and cosmic entropy, mark mortality. Death is not only the final boundary to our known existence as embodied beings; it is also the key paradigm of many other boundaries over which we make transitions as we move through life. Every shift that we make in our growth involves losing the security of the state which is being left. The earliest distinction we draw is between I and Not-I. But to take advantage of this we first have to lose our previous perception of an undifferentiated world and the security such a notion offers. We repeatedly undergo these endings until we finally come to death. And the inevitability of this experience, which cannot be experienced, is so influential that people may sometimes be so inhibited by it that they are unable to face some of these lesser endings or transitions and become neurotic.

The impulse to religious belief might be regarded as a response to this inevitable sense of loss. Faced with the reality of our mortality, the argument runs, we cast around for security. A reductionist sequence follows: religious conviction is a function of basic narcissism, concern with the self; this in turn is a response to the fear of death; reacting against this we create our gods as an infantile fantasy to enable us to cope with unfaceable reality, and this dependent stance accentuates our childlike helplessness by submission to a real or imagined leader or authority figure – God.

This 'explanation' of religion is superficial. Religious belief is not necessarily a psychologically defensive stance; it could be, and in practice may prove to be, a constructive aspect of human functioning and not compensatory [Meissner 1984]. But even if we dismiss the argument, the content remains important. Religion is indeed from some perspectives a response to human anxiety about the ending, our mortality and ultimate death, which are integral to our being created. Death strikes at the roots of our being and must make us anxious, whether we are conscious of this or not. Religious experience, therefore, is inevitably tied up with profound psychological roots. They are embedded in our unavoidable dependence, both physical and psychological, which follows from our being created. As a result, 'an authentic religious experience cannot achieve meaningful integrity without reviving the psychological roots that establish the possibility of trust on a higher level of spiritual maturity' [Meissner 1984, 130].

b) History and dependence

In common human experience reflection on history is not a sophisticated activity. It occurs all the time as individuals or groups create or demonstrate so-called 'facts'. Events are not so much obliterated or created (although both can happen) as reordered. We long for the security that a reliable past is believed to offer. A story emerges about something that happened and provides assurance. We handle our anxieties about the present and future by reflecting on the past and unconsciously reordering it. Our here-and-now experience thus becomes a mixture of past, present and believed future. But when it dawns on us just how fragile and ambiguous this mix is, we urgently seek certainty. In the flux of everyday human experience what has been gives us a notional fixed point. But using the past in our present and as an indicator, perhaps, of the future, we distort it; in a sense, therefore, we can be said to create it.

This reordering of history is another instance of dependence. A subtle process occurs as we revalue material which is already—at least in theory—publicly available. For example, children who are displaced from their families create powerful myths about their origins. When these stories are examined they often illuminate crucial facets of that *mélange* of past, present and fantasized future experience that makes them individuals. Groups, nations and families do the same. Roots become important, and myths are woven around these to sustain assurance in the present.

Religious institutions and claims to religious experience are a specific form of such behaviour. Past, present and future are fused in religious experience, but the past tends to be held as normative, not least when there is stress in the present. In Christianity instances of this dependent reordering of history regularly reappear as fundamentalism: biblical (back to the text), ecclesiastical (back to the tradition), or charismatic (back to the original—note, not just *any*— experience). Each is used to authenticate religious life by reference to a believed security which is derived from history.

c) Fragmented experience and dependence

The third mark of mortality is the way in which the variety and different intensity of experiences fragment our sense of life as a whole. Experience is often spoken of as if it were an undifferentiated entity, although we distil particular experiences and give them different value. But the more we draw such distinctions the more unconnected our experiences become. We begin to wonder whether any coherence is possible.

One option, then, is to seek something outside us to contain the confusion on our behalf. For example, the idea of God can be used to hold together incoherent experiences and thus imply that there is hope of integration only when he himself is fully known, either in this world or the next. Coherence is an attribute of God and we trust it as the point around which to orientate the broken bits of our experience. An alternative approach may be to develop an internal ordering system. Some people may use therapy or psychoanalysis as a means to self-understanding and so give these procedures their status as quasi-religions. Others assert that all experience is relative and that incoherence is intrinsic to life. They make relativism their ordering model. We may argue about which is the best or correct way to deal with this issue, but whatever method is adopted, the aim is the same—to ward off personal dis-integration.

This sense of fragmentation is integral to common human experience. The more we reflect on what happens to us, what we do and what we feel, the more awesome becomes the way in which social systems and people relate to each other. The problem of integration is bound to be addressed through dependence, although it may be heavily disguised. For example, the pluralistic society puts a premium on individual autonomy, which emphasizes personal sincerity and integrity. But in order to achieve this it underplays the obvious fact that autonomy is not a personal attribute and that each individual is autonomous only in relation to others. So personal autonomy itself can become as fantasized a dependable object as any other—a 'god'.

The experience of such fragmentation raises the spectre of being abandoned. Without a coherent context within which to set the welter of confusions that make up our common human experience, we feel alone. That is bad enough. But then the world sometimes begins to feel hostile too. It is not that it is over against us, but, in our isolation we become introspective, we discover anew our lack of internal structure to cope with the disorientating nature of our world. This leads to an irrational fear that the world will somehow retaliate against us for our failure—unless we have some protection, we are bound to suffer retribution. These anxieties, which lie deep within us, give rise to a dependent response, which we express in dependent behaviour towards some other. This may be God or a structuring of relationships between people and things. But the aim and the effect is to make the world believably reliable and thus habitable.

d) Magic and dependence

Three marks of dependence are notable in common human experience. First, there is our wish that some dependable object should be available. In religion, for instance, it is not enough for God to be reliable; he must also be accessible to his worshippers. Second, there is a corresponding tendency to deny that we are responsible for ourselves and our actions. We try to load this on to others and to avoid our authority. We flee accountability as human beings, for our various roles (parent, child, teacher, leader, etc.), and our individual or corporate responsibility. Third, as an outcome of this interaction, we begin to believe that things can be achieved without our personal involvement and at no cost to us; somehow others will do what is necessary and we can reap the benefit. This underlies our perennial longing for magical solutions to life's complexities. The magician knows how and what to do; the audience has only to watch or participate on his terms. He produces wonders without making demands, except on our credulity, which we sacrifice willingly.

While Christianity has frequently been contrasted with magic, we should, however, recognize the propensity towards it which is encouraged by a further significant dimension to the classic of creation: it includes God's loving disposition towards his creatures. Within the dependent dynamic the notion of love can be transformed into that of a comfortable haven into which we may securely settle. God's assumed reliability then becomes benignly welcoming and it can seem a sign of spiritual maturity for us to hand over to him our personal responsibility. Response to God's love subtly turns into doing something for his benefit: we unconsciously behave as though he needs us to depend on him, so that he is reinforced as God and the world becomes safer. This religious fantasy—rarely articulated—underlies some individual piety and, in its social form, folk religion. It is the dynamic basis of apotropaic, or averting, magic, which surfaces from time to time in the idea, for example, of a votive offering. It sustains the idea of a benificent God without any need to struggle to discover what it means to be human in this world.

Four aspects of human behaviour focus in God as Creator: our need for assurance about the ultimate boundary of known life; our sense of past, present and future; our longing to find coherence for our fragmented experience; and our willing collusion with any magic which might seem to release us from responsibility. Such behaviour is easily labelled 'dependent'. But dependence is more subtle and pervasive in human life and experience even than these aspects. We are facing the primary factor of human psychology, which is given and inescapable within the created order. It permeates our behaviour as finite creatures, often sustaining fantasies that make a sense of powerlessness or childishness legitimate. But this is not a whim; dependence also represents a crucial developmental stage, which is incorporated into our continuing growth and remains part of what we are as human beings. And the fantasies which provide security and a means of coping with anxiety are fundamental attributes of our creatureliness, and not insignificant personal or social myths. Unless pastors as theologians can relate this whole area of life to God, then we are excluding a huge dimension of human experience from theological consideration.

God and the Dynamic of Dependence

Theologians and worshippers alike speak about the ways in which God and his creation 'relate' to each other. But behind that word lies a complex of ideas which needs to be clarified. Therefore, before addressing the specific question of God and dependence, we need a short excursus to clarify three terms, all rooted on 'relate'—relationship, relatedness and inter-relation.

Relationship describes links between persons. It implies self-giving, as one person takes an initiative or responds to another. It is widely employed both in theology and pastoral ministry. It characterizes a view of God which gives prominence to divine grace—God's self-giving and self-disclosure. Relationship stresses mutuality, since in any relationship both parties must be capable of responding to each other.

Relatedness, by contrast, describes how people relate to each other through their different roles and how they connect with concepts, ideas and stances. So, for example, when we think of the human race as a sub-system within the larger system of creation, the connection between God and human beings is appropriately described in terms of their relatedness. This does not mean that the creature somehow has two parts, one capable of relationship and the other only of relatedness. The language simply makes clearer the type of relating that predominates at any moment.

Thirdly, there is *interrelation*. This ungainly word acknowledges that connections between people, whether as persons or in role, whether relationship or relatedness, are always reciprocal. A series of complicated dynamics can be discerned between persons or between an individual and a group. Within the individual, too, dialogue takes place between his person and his role. The word 'interrelation' reminds us of the obvious, but easily overlooked, point that, in addition to whatever the relationship and relatedness between two people or groups may be, the fact of their relating itself has an effect. It creates a new context which affects those involved and others.

An example may make these distinctions clearer. Take a father and his daughter. Between them there is a *relationship*, a maturing person-to-person contact in which each is affirmed by the other through love. Looking from another perspective, however, we can discern a *relatedness* between them in a social context. They occupy roles, father and daughter, to which certain responsibilities attach. Further, however, their *interrelation* creates a context which affects them and others, chiefly members of the family, but also a wider range of people with whom they are in touch.

We may now return to the question of God and dependence. The longing that someone should be dependable is expressed in the demand that they should be immediately available. We desire the dependable object, whoever or whatever that may be, to be unfailingly on hand to do what is needed. We may contrast this dependent attitude with independence and dismiss it as immature. But when we assume that independence is the mark of personal maturity, we oversimplify matters by excluding a third possibility: mature life is marked by the confident exercise of autonomy based upon satisfactory management of dependence. Immature dependence—the longing to be relieved of responsibility for our lives and the wish for magical solutions—locks us into questions of relationship alone. We become preoccupied with how dependable our partner—whether God or a fellow human being—is and less concerned with what we might achieve together. Mature behaviour in the context of such dependence, however, puts greater reliance on relatedness: we still value people for who they are but emphasize our mutual responsibilities, which derive from our distinctive roles.

When relationship and relatedness are both employed, a person may then become sufficiently confident to explore the complex interrelations between him, the world and others. But two conditions must be fulfilled if such a quality of living is to be achieved: first, we need the security of being aware of our role; and second, we also need the personal assurance which comes from being able to acknowledge our dependence.

Examples will make the importance of these distinctions clearer and indicate their significance for theological thinking. One is drawn from human development and the other from the biblical tradition.

First take a child. As she grows she shifts with increasing confidence and competence between being dependent and autonomous. Sometimes she is more dependent, sometimes more autonomous. But her growth in maturity is disclosed as she progressively understands that she really lives in interdependence with her mother and others. Realizing this, a good mother knows that the child needs to be encouraged to move away from and back to her. This shows in public behaviour as the child runs to and from mother. But this represents an internal process of oscillation as she progressively orders her world by risky development and comforting regression. If she is to become adult she needs increasingly to claim her autonomy. But in order to achieve this desirable aim she also has to be able from time to time securely to regress to her original felt dependence, both for reassurance but also to enable her to reflect upon the restructuring of herself which is what we call growth. She does not leave dependence behind; she uses it differently. A mother's job is to manage the conditions so that her daughter can both move to independence and regress to dependence. Such managed regression is crucial; without it exploration of autonomy produces anxiety, making us less confident in facing the next demand, whether as child or adult.

Or, secondly, take stories of people meeting God, especially as they appear in the Old Testament. Although each encounter is different, there are usually three discernible phases to them. For example, when Moses comes upon the burning bush (Exod. 3.1 – 12), each phase is clear: first, he is not surprisingly unsure in the presence of God or his emissary (3.6); second, God gives some command or announces a decision (3.10); third, God and Moses then negotiate what they intend jointly to achieve (3.11 – 12). Falling in awe, the human partner attributes all power to God and little or none to himself. He impotently adopts a posture from which he can contribute nothing. The second phase shifts him away from this personal *relationship* towards a sense of *relatedness*. By giving a command God assigns him his role as creature and confirms his authority as such. On that basis man and God are each established in roles which enable genuine and usable contact to take place. Once that is affirmed, negotiation, or *interrelationship*, begins and achievement ensues. We see here, as with human development, the shift from dependence to creative interdependence and the importance of managed regression. In these stories it is managed as God first accepts his human creature's fear and awe and transforms it by shifting the ground of the encounter through the personal affirmation of relationship to the more task-orientated dimension of relatedness.

Each of these illustrations, drawn from very different sources, shows that the primitive side of our human dependence cannot be disregarded. If God engages with us at the level of mature dependence alone, requiring articulated response and rational behaviour, this will not do. This assumption usually lies behind the general use of the word 'relate' in both theological and pastoral contexts. But it limits theologians and leads to some of the frustrations that many ministers, especially those who are theologically acute, experience in their pastoral work.

For example, we have noted that reliability is an essential ingredient in creation. Its order is the outworking of coherence in God himself. This sense of relatedness to our context is the foundation on which we have built both our scientific view of the world and our theological explorations. Reliability, order and relatedness with their attention to interrelation, address aspects of *mature* dependence and how it may be harnessed for creativity. But God's engagement with his creation cannot be confined to this one facet of dependence. What of the *immature* dependence which is also a mark of our human experience and behaviour? It cannot be ignored on the grounds of irrelevance or a belief that people do or should grow out of it. The psychodynamically informed view of human life shows that we do not grow out of it. Indeed it is frequently manifested in religion. One way, therefore, to approach this complex but deeply felt issue could be through this question: What is the significance of the phenomenon of religion for the doctrine of creation?

Dependence, Religion and Creation

Pastors know that working with dependence is like swimming in a lake of glue. Religious leaders and simple believers meet this in their dealings with popular or folk religion: no sooner do you think that you have extricated yourself than you are trapped again. This is basic assumption dependence in a pure form: the wish for magic; the irrational hope that results may be achieved without personal commitment; profound anger when they are not; and a persistent expectation, which sometimes amounts to demand, that God should be immediately effective. Pastors are generally suspicious of this sort of religion and on the whole theologians do not take it seriously into account. Those who have difficulty in living with the reality of this immature dependence, whether in themselves or others, may sometimes in the interests of faith seek to discount religious experience as data.

But no one engaged in pastoral ministry can go along with such polarizing. That is to ignore, or even discard, a major area of human behaviour with which we live. Pastors have to take a theologically more positive view of religion and claims to religious experience. When Feuerbach and Freud criticized religion as a particular instance of projective behaviour they were offering a reasonably accurate interpretation of some dimensions of religion. This scarcely needs to be discussed when we look at the evidence around us and in ourselves. But their further restriction of the discussion of what that evidence may signify must, however, be discounted. We need not worry about the answer to the question: Is God a projection of human need for a father figure? The crucial issue for the theologian and pastor is functional and arises within the stance of experimental faith: What is the significance of the projections and fantasies about a divine father figure for our concept of God?

The first question implies that religious believers construct a fantasy world which suits their dependent needs and so relieves their anxieties. There is little point in responding to such a view with ideas of reasonable religion and rational faith. What lies behind the question is not amenable to articulate argument. It raises the issue of ineradicable dependence, from which there is no escape — nor should there be a desire for escape. In firm believer, half-believer and sceptic alike there is a persistent feeling of suspicion that there is something in the suggestion because it addresses something primary in us as a result of our being created. Reason alone, therefore, cannot speak to this question. The pastor as theologian presses a different issue: given this dependence, immature and mature, what creative use of it might God make? Because this dynamic runs powerfully through our individual and corporate life, God, if he is to be the ultimate referent for religious experience, may be expected somehow to acknowledge this behaviour and reveal how he is prepared to meet us in it.

Worship, that characteristically religious (though not specifically Christian) activity, comes to mind. In worship people claim to encounter God. Worshippers place themselves consciously in the context of God and offer adoration. But in so doing they do not function solely at the rational level of mature dependence. Worship is also a way of making immature dependence sufficiently conscious for us to harness it to our way of living. The postures adopted, for instance, demonstrate this. And the claim that we offer all of life in worship may be more true than we had hitherto realized. People take part in order to reaffirm, and have reaffirmed, their autonomy as God's creatures and so resume a life of deliberate interrelation with God and their contexts. The traditional Christian description of this is 'our neighbour'; and as a result of worship, life with him, her or them may become marked by confident interdependence [Reed 1978].

We need to match this practical interpretation (which we shall examine further below) to the theological question of why God might expect the worship of his creation. Part of the answer to that is that we are like this by virtue of our creation and our inevitable dependence. We contribute to creating a supernatural figure, and in worshipping it (her or him) address aspects of ourselves. But we cannot end the matter there. As we have begun to see, while dependent behaviour is a significant ingredient of what it means to be human, dependence is a complex aspect of ourselves. We may identify the immature dependence, which is seen in the longing for a 'god' and worship of him. But because of the multifaceted dimensions of human dependence, it is a mistake in a religious context to consider only one type of this—immature dependence. We cannot deal with the evidence for this without examining the significance of mature dependence.

The theological question has also to be taken further. It has generally been shaped in terms of God and creation. But the way this is done in fact restricts the range of examination. That is why few, if any, religions stop there. Belief in God and an ordered creation are fundamental, but religious people discover that their experience continually pulls them beyond the stage of merely affirming order. Religious language reflects experience. It is not full of indicatives alone. It is the language of the subjunctive (what might be) and the optative (what we wish could be). Therefore we find in our Judaeo-Christian tradition that no doctrine of creation is complete without some corresponding idea of new creation.

In the Christian scheme this becomes the classic of the resurrection. We must turn to this before we can bring together dependence as a whole, both immature and mature. For if with this classic we enter the world of fantasy and imagination, which is one dimension of our dependent stance as creatures, we can do so only within particular parameters. Or, to put it another way, although the idea of God as Creator seems to be common to religion, it is not affirmed apart from some specific belief which gives it content that can be experienced. In Judaism, for example, this content may be the continuing survival of the people of God. In Christianity, however, it is the doctrine of the new creation or resurrection.

Note

1   For a note on 'regression', see p. 218. The term is widely employed, both in strict senses (which are not always compatible) and more generally. It describes reversion to earlier, or basic, forms of development that are not left behind as we grow but which remain forever part of us. The word 'regression' is therefore not used pejoratively, and should not be read as such.

TWELVE

The Classic of the Resurrection

The resurrection remains central and controversial. It draws together four main strands of the Christian faith. First, although the notion of a special event seems to contradict the coherence implied by creation, the resurrection is held to be a similar act of divine initiative. Second, resurrection cannot be construed apart from the life and death of Jesus. When, as happens from time to time, the resurrection is divorced from the crucifixion, it then in effect annuls rather than confirms the way of the cross. Third, this classic includes a future reference: the resurrection does not mark the end of the Jesus saga but is the point at which the consummation of all things begins. And, fourthly, people have persistently found, however often the logic of the argument is questioned, that Jesus' resurrection in some way witnesses to personal survival after death.

These four stances are still present in contemporary dispute. The idea of the resurrection itself seems to challenge the coherence of the world on which we construct our lives, including our scientific thought. It feels easier and appears more reasonable to change our belief than to restructure the whole world and our ways of thinking. A second issue concerns knowledge of God. If his revealed self lies beyond our usual definitions of rationality, then the common ground on which religious experience and theological thinking are founded crumbles. What sort of interchange can occur between people and God, if each inhabits such a different world of reason that communication is impossible? Religious and reasonable people alike find that they cannot live within the Christian tradition. The third question is that of a unique event. There is nothing intrinsically odd about such an idea; in a sense every event is unique. But in a religious context, where believers claim the uniqueness of the resurrection,

184

such a tenet becomes impossible. It seems to destroy any sense that God might be accessible to us and that we might be able to discourse with him.

Around these foci rage debate and argument. But none of them can be isolated from the experience of the religious person. They concern our knowledge of ourselves and of our world; whether God can be known; and, even if he can, whether there can be any interchange with him. Much work has been done on the philosophical, historical and textual questions concerning the resurrection. But since it also raises issues about the dynamics of human behaviour, we should see what illumination we might gain if we adopt a perspective based on that.

Some Contemporary Theoretical Stances

a) Elegance

As we approach the end of the twentieth century, ideas of imagination and beauty are once more being increasingly acknowledged in the notion of elegance. We leap back behind the massive edifice of nineteenth-century thought to recover the idea of order in relation to form. For example, exploration of our universe goes in two congruent directions: outwards to the vastness of space and inwards into the microcosmic particles of matter. Hypotheses, especially those that seek unifying theories for both explorations, are elaborated in terms of elegance and beauty [Davies 1984]. What we know of the way our brains work seems to complement this emphasis. In the interaction between the hemispheres, one is chiefly concerned with logical thought and the other with imaginative creativity [Blakeslee 1980]. Symmetry is required for intellectual and artistic creation.

This stress on balance and elegance can stimulate thinking on the resurrection. We might consider it in terms of the symmetry that it represents within the divine scheme of things. God's achievement lies in the way that he confirms the elegance of his creation by aligning imaginative creativity — a new creation — with the logical order of the coherent universe — creation itself. Beauty and elegance can be contemplated and even adored. But they also have a function, which is best described as heuristic [Polya 1945]. The use of elegance in the face of intractable problems presented by logical thought can circumvent the block. Instead of building an argument step by logical step from the base upwards, we make connections which seem and feel right, but which we cannot wholly justify, and so construct the superstructure and test how we may then build down to the foundation. In Judaeo-Christian thought this connection between elegance, beauty and creativity permeates Wisdom [Crenshaw 1982], a tradition that can also inform practical pastoral behaviour [Campbell 1981].

b) Openness of Fields

A second point concerns the way that knowledge and understanding connect at different, but compatible, levels. Here we employ the notion of openness of fields. This theory argues that in any complex organization each separate system must be open both upwards and downwards. It is open downwards in the sense that it must co-ordinate with certain basic statements; no system can start its own life out of the blue. But it is also open upwards in the sense that it cannot contain all its consequences; it is a means of serving a greater end. This implies that no formalized system of thought can be both consistent and complete at the same time [Torrance 1969; Torrance 1976]. We can regard the creation as one such complex organization, interpreted through a whole range of different schemes of understanding. One of these consists of theological affirmations, based upon people's belief; another may be composed of historical statements. The link between theological affirmations and historical statements is not optional; however different in status, they must connect.

The resurrection offers a particular instance of how this theory applies. Without both personal affirmation and history—the order in which they come does not matter—there is no classic of the resurrection. By trying to think about the resurrection in the context of this theory of open fields, we discover that it is not a matter of private religious discourse but concerns human knowledge in general. This classic has to be articulated in terms which are compatible with interpretations of the common human experience of our world.

We have to think of it in the setting of the larger field of creation. As a result, if we wish to claim that what we profess is complete, then it must be inconsistent. Alternatively, if we wish to stress its consistency, then we shall have to acknowledge that what we say is going to be incomplete. Our inevitable dependence, especially for that certainty which we immaturely expect, urges us not to recognize these obvious points. It demands both consistency and completion, and presses any who profess a belief in the resurrection magically to resolve the dilemma.

c) Story

Thirdly, we note the renewed prominence that is being given to story and narrative for the development of faith. We use stories to make connections between our past and the present. Their evocative power stimulates responses and the involving side of story conveys information. Thus they transform us when we make these stories our own. There is nothing remarkable about this. The procedure of constructing and using stories lies, for example, at the heart of psychoanalysis and its various derivatives. The patient constructs a story, which is not history—the past—but is the past and present combined to create an interpretative story. The past is not recovered; it is used in the present to construct a way of interpreting life now [Schafer 1978]. Or to take another instance, a social-worker may try to work with a fostered or adopted child by creating together a scrapbook of known bits of their life as a way of helping them locate themselves in the world. Again, this does not construct history; it generates enough of a story, which the child may use as a means of sorting himself or herself out.

The resurrection narratives are stories in this sense. When we read and hear them, we can discern qualitatively different material from the pre-crucifixion stories of Jesus. The most significant difference lies in the way that the role of the hearer as one who contributes to the message being conveyed is made explicitly plain. The characters in the stories create the story itself. This is not about *either* Jesus *or* his disciples, but about the interaction between them. Neither alone creates the narrative; it stands as a product of their dealing with each other. If we extract one or the other, the story collapses. Therefore, there is no account of the resurrection itself—a point which the gospel writers all emphasize. There are only stories about appearances, and an appearance is generated as much by those who receive it as by those who provide it.

When we begin to discuss the resurrection, whatever the terms, the issues seem to become depressingly over-complex. However, from these technical questions, with which we are today confronted, a fact which is of crucial importance to the pastor emerges: when dealing with this classic, we are not in the realm of rational human behaviour alone. Much effort has been expended in trying to make the doctrine amenable to our rational minds. Some argue that in the story of Jesus Christ we can hear the call to personal decision only when we recognize that the historical detail lies beyond recovery. That frees us to believe, to act and to research. Others present the resurrection as a historical event, open to scrutiny and providing evidence that demands faith. Yet others regard it as a powerful symbol within the framework of the history of religion. By contrast with this universal symbol of human hope, the resurrection has also been promoted as a description of intense personal experience. And finally to these we may add the bolder approach which argues that within the prevailing view of history the resurrection is improbable, if not inconceivable. Christians, therefore, need to redefine what is meant by 'history', so that, by using the category of apocalyptic, the resurrection becomes the norm.

The difficulties are strongly felt, but the proffered solutions seem to take us away from the world of everyday human experience. They fail to deal with our felt longings about God (or some such being), which become explicit in religious experience, essentially because they are too rational. We have already seen that dependence is a complex dynamic that includes within it aspects of ourselves which lie deeper than rationality.

Resurrection and Curiosity

When we think of common human experience, and of religious experience in particular, we include the significance of the irrational aspect to life. This is not a weakness to be therapeutized away, but a facet of our selves that can be recognized and used. But if it is ignored, it may return in bizarre ways. This is certainly true of its religious manifestations. And in thinking about the classic of the resurrection we are in an area where the rational and irrational appear to coincide. These are complex issues which are illuminated by a specific appreciation of curiosity.

Creation's order stimulates our curiosity. It invites us to struggle to extend the frontiers of our knowledge. Whatever the modern disillusion with science, our era remains one of curiosity, which, largely because of the easy availability of the media, is no longer restricted to a few. But this curiosity is not confined to our interest in the world around us. It is also a critical factor in the way that we develop as individuals and relate to one another in families and other social groups. Families where members display delinquent behaviour also frequently show a lack of interpersonal curiosity. People seem to prefer not to know about each other or their relationships: 'These family members are often extraordinarily certain that they know, understand, and can speak for the experience of other members of the family without further discussion or question' [Shapiro 1982a, 69]. Inquiry and interest is replaced by a certainty which is pathological. Believing that there is no need to ask about one another and what is going on between them, the members find that their relations with each other atrophy. Relationships become fixed, as do the pathological symptoms which the individuals display:

> The continuing capacity of the parent to tolerate ambivalence, ambiguity and uncertainty, and to maintain an attitude of openness and curiosity about the child's experience, is an important element in the healthy psychological growth of the child. . . . A relationship is demonstrated between so-called 'pathological certainty' and the subjective experiences of isolation, emptiness and futility that dominate family life in these disturbed families. [Shapiro 1982a, 87]

Such curiosity, theologically speaking, is a key ingredient in the classic of creation and new creation when we consider its negative side—sin. The Church today does not speak very cogently about this. We may blame this in part on changes in our world-view and in part on the way that in the Western tradition sin has largely been confined to the life of the individual. Today, however, we are more aware of being sinned against than sinning. People live with a powerful, but usually unclear, sense of impotence in the face of 'them'.

However, by taking the notion of curiosity the pastor can recover an approach to sin which emphasizes its intrinsic place in creation and, therefore, also in new creation or resurrection. We can enlarge this idea of curiosity as a vital function from family roles to those that each person has, for example, as a citizen or as a human being within God's creation. Whatever the context and the corresponding role, we are inclined to make the same bedevilling assumption, that we *know* about each other — 'pathological certainty'.

This emerges in our easy claims to understanding. For example, a radio counsellor described his work as enabling those who phoned in to 'understand what was going on inside them' (*sic*), a good example of pathological certainty. The client and the counsellor publicly colluded to assume that such understanding is possible in order to avoid the obvious point that it is impossible to understand other people's behaviour, and probably not even your own. We might risk interpretation, but that, as we have seen, is another thing altogether from understanding.

This assumption of certainty, that understanding is possible, constitutes sin. If this condition of human life is left unexposed, pathological assumptions are made which are themselves debilitating. This is illustrated, for example, by one myth of the fall. Adam and Eve assume knowledge about each other's lives, their relationship with each other, and their relatedness in their roles as human creatures to God the Creator. They do not need to explore because they make this assumption. As a result, their whole life is corrupted — their personal relationship with each other, their intimacy with God, their individual selves and their relatedness to the world. Without curiosity we become less than human and less competent at taking up roles. The result is that communal and individual pathologies increase.

In family therapy, from which this insight about curiosity originates, the first work is at the parents' capacity to tolerate ambiguity and uncertainty. If they can recover this, other members of the family may become able to reorientate their inner worlds and so develop a new style of relating to each other. They begin to admit that they do not in fact understand another person's feelings, but that through participation they can appreciate enough of their own to be useful to others. Gradually a new discovery is made: what happens between members of a family not only affects them; it affects other members and thus there reappears the genuine unit—the family.

This process throws valuable light on the idea of the resurrection. If we grasp that the essence of sin is the absence of curiosity, then salvation occurs in so far as this capacity is restored to us. For that to happen to creatures the first response has to be from the Creator, who proves himself willing to tolerate ambiguity and uncertainty about himself and can be believed to do so. The classic of creation, with its emphasis on coherence and rationality, and its demand for mature dependence on the part of the creature in relation to the Creator, is by itself inadequate to support such an idea. For it does not sufficiently address our immature dependence. This, however, is what we find being handled when we turn to the new creation or resurrection.

The resurrection stands within the Christian faith as the place where God acknowledges our immature dependence and the irrational behaviour that is often connected with it as a significant facet of the human soul and one which he considers worth stimulating and investing in. The stories, as well as the idea itself, emphasize ambiguity and have always aroused correspondingly ambivalent responses in disciples, from the time of the New Testament to the present day. There is a naughtiness about the whole idea, as if what ought not to happen does, and a playfulness about the stories. The confines of order, or of pathological certainty, are broken by God's quizzical invitation to be curious. This is not the so-called detached curiosity of the scientific observer, but the intimate curiosity of human relations, which directs us to interrelationships. We cannot separately interpret ourselves or others; we can only interpret both and explore how they connect for the benefit of each.

This process exposes to us the significance of our irrational selves, an experience which is fraught with risk but is ultimately humanizing. The resurrection cannot be examined in terms of reason alone. Our rational selves seek understanding of our lives, the world—even of God. But there are also the parts of ourselves about which we can only risk interpretation. These draw us nearer the edge of existence, where our rational selves seem less all-embracing and significant, and our feelings, irrational when thought about but essential for our being ourselves, take over.

Even when allowance is made for the wide range of possible interpretations, this classic arouses particularly fierce passions and divisions. There are those who believe most firmly, and those who will not believe at all. The resurrection polarizes belief; believers and unbelievers alike respond. Few remain completely agnostic, although sometimes this excuse may be offered for vacillation. But these divisions are not solely between believers and non-believers. Within the believer (and maybe also in the unbeliever) there is a split between the dependent longing ('If only God would do something sure and dramatic') and the need to test reality which derives from faith in God the Creator ('God does not demonstrate his presence by miracles of this type'). Both feelings are aroused by the idea of resurrection and complement each other. The resurrection, therefore, is both professed by the committed believer and is a focal point for unbelief. But it is also the theological means by which we begin to value such unbelief, since the believer's questions are not peculiar to him or her. They are instances of basic human experience—dependent longing for the irrational sides of ourselves to be affirmed and the need for rational testing of reality—and the tension that these two facets generate.

This is important for the pastor as he struggles to link his distinctively Christian faith to the folk beliefs of those among whom he ministers. The two are not separated by any test of belief in the resurrection. This core tenet of the faith, however, can now be seen as the specific point of contact which God provides for that immature dependence which is the mark of folk religion. The classic of the resurrection is therefore not a private Christian subject; it deals with issues which lie at the core of common human experience.

First, an essential foundation of human life—curiosity, which is of the essence of common human experience—

emerges at the heart of the Christian confession. One of the marks which defines that faith — the resurrection of Jesus Christ — turns out to be a focal affirmation both for religious experience and confession and for common human experience. The interpretation of everyday life in the light of the gospel is the pastor's task. Here is a primary point of contact for such interpretation, provided that he can escape the restricting tyranny of rationality, whether in himself, his fellow Christians or in those with whom he is ministering. With his feelings, therefore (and consequentially his irrational parts), he can begin to make and use connections between his distinctively Christian profession, which motivates him, and the expectations and demands which people might make. If these connections fail, then, as with the absence of curiosity — or, as we might say, with sin — the unities of creation are destroyed, not least the way that men and women of every and any persuasion have life in common to explore. When the resurrection becomes the private concern of the believer, it also ceases to be a life-sustaining classic and becomes a point of internal controversy. And for the rest of the world a story, which exposes the importance to God of both the irrational parts of ourselves and our immature dependence, is made inaccessible.

Second, the resurrection is the way in which God creates the conditions for working on this needful curiosity. It introduces imbalance into whatever secure stance any of us may have adopted. By encouraging curiosity about God and ourselves, believers or unbelievers, the resurrection creates a disturbance which can produce change. It will not allow us to escape to the haven of rationality or of irrational behaviour alone. Here we meet the dynamic equivalent of the heuristic process of discovery. The tension between these complementary facets of our being is recognized in the resurrection, but not resolved. Curiosity in families is stimulated and made creative by encouraging participation. Similarly the resurrection does not allow detached observation; it is not amenable as event alone. Nor, however, can it be sustained as a notion which has its origins in the believer alone. This is why it is impossible precisely to locate the issue of the resurrection. It is neither wholly outside the believer (a matter of investigation) nor wholly inside, but both inside and outside and at the boundary of our experience. This is exactly, but not surprisingly, given the topic, the description of a transitional object, which we saw earlier is an illuminating way of thinking about God himself (see pp. 21—4).

When, therefore, we proclaim the resurrection, we are offering neither magic nor something accessible to reason. This classic represents the claim that God endorses that necessary curiosity which runs through our being. For the pastor, the debilitation which results from the denial of such pervasive curiosity—sin—is daily manifested in the lives of those with whom he deals. But the central tenet of his faith, the classic of the resurrection, does not stand apart from this core dilemma of human life. On the contrary, it affirms that this creation is not only sustained by order and kept explorable by reason but is also enlivened by curiosity and the imaginative use of ourselves.

Common human experience, therefore, points the pastor to his central belief; his central belief refers him back to the heart of common human experience. This is the frequently described daily experience of ministry. But it now becomes manifestly congruent with a core Christian classic—the resurrection. In our pastoring, then, we are not dealing with the dynamics of human behaviour alone. We are discovering in the process itself part of God's interpretation of our human life at its unconscious level.

Resurrection and Play

In our thinking about creation we can become so preoccupied with creativity and its results that we overlook the important dimension of play. Play is not confined to children. We all play when we act without discernible conscious motive or concern for a specific end. Play is performed for its own sake and carries its own value, 'the resolution of a dialectic between work and rest' [Wainwright 1980, 26]. Our undisclosed selves become momentarily discernible as we unselfconsciously express what we are through relaxation rather than by purposeful application: 'Play is paradoxical behaviour. Exploring what is familiar, practising what has already been mastered, friendly aggression, sex without coition, excitement about nothing, social behaviour not defined by specific common activity or by social structure, pretence not intended to deceive: this is play' [Millar 1968, 255—6].

The resurrection narratives about the risen Christ are shot through with enigma and play. The empty tomb poses a riddle which persists throughout the history of the Church: 'Where is Jesus?' This is not a simple question requiring a single answer, but one which puts a supplementary demand on the enquirer: 'Where do you expect him to be?' or 'Where would you like him to be?' It is also worth reminding ourselves that the bulk of the material in the Gospels is not about the resurrection, but is in the form of encounter stories between individuals, groups and the risen Christ. These stories, far from being incontrovertible evidence of the risen Christ, are marked by the disciples' ignorance and blindness. They seem to have little intrinsic value as evidence of more than that. But when we realize that they are describing play, they take on new power. Mary meeting the gardener is caught up in the twists of disguises and charades. The walkers on the road to Emmaus take part in the old game of blind man's buff. The confused behaviour of the group of disciples is exactly that of people caught between work and rest—i.e. at play. Angels and messages, appearances and confusion signify that the resurrection narratives are set in the sphere of games and play.

The concept of play again carries us beyond the realm of rational, consciously purposeful behaviour. We naturally need to beware of idealizing it. Like any other human activity, it takes place in the context of life and is not itself all of living [Sutton-Smith & Kelly 1984]. Nevertheless, this dimension to our experience reminds us that it is as mistaken to limit inquiry into the resurrection to what 'actually' happened, as it is to try and interpret our play and games, whether as adults or children, with the same restricted question. Our questions must be framed so as to admit answers which can include the irrational as well as the rational aspects to God's activity. If either of these facets is absent, God's engagement with us as we are will inevitably be inadequate.

The classic of creation presents God as a reliable focus for our legitimately dependent expectations. We are the creatures who look to our Creator. The new creation, with its ambiguities and tensions, demonstrates that we are not

confined to that dependent mode but are made with it so that
we may harness it to work with God. To bring this about God
meets our dependent expectation at our most primitive
unconscious level, where magic is sought. What is more, he
further invites us to see him as he expresses through play
new sides to his inner being. The question: 'What sort of God
is it that raises Jesus from the dead?' does not now have to be
answered solely in terms of the coherence of the universe.

Creative partnership with God sounds wonderful but feels
beyond many of us, not least the ordinary pastor and
Christian. But sharing in play is not. God reveals himself in
an activity which is an end in itself and without ulterior
motives. This is the activity in which he invites us to be his
partners and in so doing discloses that our destiny, too, is
play. No longer can we consider this aspect of life a pastime;
it is the purpose for which we are created. We are invited to
exist, like God himself, between work and rest, where we
may truly claim that we are most obviously what we are
made to be. Work is necessary as an alliance with the Creator
God; rest is desirable, to sustain perspective. But between
the two we play, bringing the seriousness of reality and the
range of our imagination into a harmony that generates new
life in us and for others. A revitalized sense of the dynamics
of play in the resurrection gives new depth to a major question
of our existence. This, as phrased in the opening question of
the Shorter Catechism of Westminster (1648), is: 'What is
the chief end of man?' The answer remains, even if expounded
in new terms: 'Man's chief end is to glorify God and to enjoy
him for ever.'

The resurrection invites our involvement, calling us like
children to be caught up in this specific instance of God's
play. A delicate touch is needed to turn dependence to useful
work. In a dependent group, for example, the leader cannot
deny members' expectations. If he does, destructive anger,
either as violence or apathy, results. Equally he cannot merely
endorse the dependence, since that reinforces its stultifying
effect. The skill is to find the means to indicate that it is a
necessary but debilitating condition. One effective way of
doing this is through humour: the oblique comment can be
more effective than the direct description. It acknowledges

the dependence and simultaneously skews perceptions and thus brings about change.

Just these qualities are found in the God of the classic of the resurrection. There is a quizzical, humorous quality to the accounts which also marks the concept of resurrection itself. By providing this classic, in which our necessary curiosity can be stimulated and exercised, God enables us to live with the questions of magic which our dependent longings produce. These are the 'What if . . . ?' questions of life, which show by their form their origins in dependence. But the resurrection, while encouraging the dependent question, refuses to allow us escape to magical answers. It asks the further question: 'What if such a thing did and does happen?' In so doing it forces us to address our many dependencies, wherever they appear in aspects of our lives, not only in our religious beliefs.

The fundamental dynamic of our humanity—dependence, both mature and immature—is obliquely, tantalizingly and humorously interpreted by this act. Inviting ultimate trust, God affirms that he is beyond us, offers us a point of supportive and affectionate recourse, and demonstrates that his vitality is free of our contribution. Because we are invited to share in this playing, we are driven to examine our internal world of created objects, including the God upon whom we each project. We can discover that God is not an hallucination, but one about whom we have to take a position. But, finally, we can realistically appreciate that his fate is to be relegated to limbo by most people, including at times ourselves or, at least, ourselves in part.

We earlier encountered the unfamiliar idea of God as a transitional object, like that teddy bear, frequently discarded but rarely, if ever, lost entirely (see pp. 21 − 4). In the classic of the resurrection this notion re-emerges, but now at the heart of the Christian faith, not at the periphery of generalized belief. It is not a degenerate form of religion, but one of the essentials of our life as creatures of God.

Resurrection and Folk Religion

This last point brings us to the theological significance of folk religion. The demand for ritual expression of confused, dimly felt, but none the less real, feelings is one which every pastor knows. Some regard it as residual or debased religion and argue that it is best ignored. But apart from being pastorally unwise, that stance is theologically damaging to the gospel. Folk religion has a theological function. By presenting us with belief in a God whom they had consigned to limbo, those who manifest folk religion take us to the heart of the classics of creation and new creation. The expressions of folk religion consistently direct us to the dimension of God's nature that has emerged from our behaviourally informed reflection on the resurrection.

Because dependence is an integral part of creation, people in general, albeit for the most part unwittingly, need believers and churches to sustain the possibility of belief in the continuing liveliness of God. Because churches, ministers and believers are available, they allow others to recall, as needed, the God they have relegated to limbo. But this recovery is not casual. There is bewilderingly intense feeling, often of possession and control, when people find churches or believers inadequate or unsuitable for this task. It surfaces when, for example the closure of a church building is announced or when a minister (for whom the generic term becomes 'vicar') is believed to have refused to baptize a baby.

The converse, however, may be less obvious: religious believers need those who have left God in limbo but who also retain in their make-up as dependent creatures something that we can characterize as religious experience. Otherwise they may, in their sophisticated believing, overlook the irrational dimension to religious belief in themselves as well as in those with whom they are dealing. Some of the problems that ministers face lie precisely here: they become closed to these aspects of their own life and belief, and so cannot be sufficiently open to them in others. What is for the minister a minor facet of belief, can be for others the whole scenario.

The classic of the resurrection is central to the Christian faith; it is not, however, confined to the belief of the Church. This distinctive confession addresses a side of human behaviour that is fundamental for all, believer and unbeliever alike. This implies that the problems which we associate intellectually and emotionally with the doctrine of the resurrection should be kept as problems and not solved or explained. If we try to do this, however noble the reason, we excuse ourselves from facing basic dependence and so deny people the opportunity of discovering both that God engages with it and how he does so for them.

The question of the empty tomb is the key instance. Some wish to turn God into the magician of the resurrection by having him perform a major miracle. The resurrection is always in danger of appearing to be a magical trick, as God does something incredible and unique. This might not be too serious, except that it also assumes that he does this apart from any involvement on our part. It is his act alone and we are merely those who believe in it or contemplate it. If we take this view, then we have uncritically used the empty tomb to sustain our dependent longings. The story is then stuck in that particular dynamic, and it cannot function in any useful way, either for ourselves or, more importantly, to inform the pastoral and evangelistic ministry of the Church.

Another way of looking at this question, however, is to see that arguments for and against the tomb being empty represent identical wishes to avoid the internal anxiety that the ambiguity of the evidence for the resurrection arouses. Each assured conclusion—that it was empty, that it was not, that we cannot know—is a slide into immature dependence upon an unambiguous God. Either he does miracles, or he does not, or he remains beyond examination. But whichever position is adopted, it feels reliable to its proponent and gives a sense of security. Yet one stance is in fact no more mature or sophisticated than any other, since none of them allows the classic of the resurrection to function to interpret us out of our innate tendency towards reassurance of some kind. The controversy, therefore, for all its apparent cunning and sophistication, may merely keep us, believer and unbeliever alike, in an immaturely dependent and uncreative state.

The story of the empty tomb is a means by which God encounters our dependence, whatever form it takes. This may be our longing for magic in God, which, as we have seen, is faced by the stories but with which there is no collusion. It may be a desire to be assured about our fate after death: does the resurrection guarantee future life or does it assure us that we do not survive? The former has on the whole been the historic Christian belief, the latter becoming more prominent in recent years. The empty tomb confirms neither, but it does direct us, as a tomb, to the mortality which is a reality to be faced by all. What is more, this story addresses our dependence in that playful, humorous, but finally interpretatively serious, fashion that we have discerned in the whole complex of the resurrection.

The crucial question about the story of the empty tomb, therefore, is how it is brought to bear on whatever activity, new discovery or exploration that is required in our lives or for others at any moment. It is most faithfully dealt with when we set it in the context of how we experience in ourselves and, so far as we can be aware, in others, the way that God acknowledges our dependent needs and interprets them into change and new life.

When we claim that God meets us at the level of our unconscious life, we include in this that he takes seriously the dependence with which we are imbued. This is how the central tenet of the resurrection and the fringe beliefs represented by folk religion are held together. There is an interaction which too sophisticated a solution or belief destroys. If believers lose the innocence of the folk-religious aspects of themselves by rejecting them in others, they will also find that they have lost the transforming power of the new creation. In the resurrection of Jesus God copes with the dependent feelings of his creation in such a way as to encourage work with him to continue. Our longing for magic is focused and expressed, but is not allowed to dominate. The resurrection meets our desire for magic without becoming magical. We cannot discard the sense of wonder, but equally this proves inadequate as the sole basis of our life in God's creation.

Conclusion

We should not isolate the resurrection within the nexus of Christian classics—creation, incarnation, crucifixion and resurrection. It is the most broadening of them all, because in creation and resurrection (new creation) God handles that pervasive dependence which undergirds all our existence. Incarnation and crucifixion are primarily concerned with God's work and his invitation to us to co-operate with him.

But creation and resurrection concern other dimensions, which have no discernible end or result. Incarnation produces the Kingdom of God and its demand, which Christians focus through prayer. Crucifixion demonstrates the way in which that demand is to be lived and orders our spiritual life. But by contrast creation and new creation (resurrection) endorse activities which lack obvious purpose—self-giving in play, celebration and joy. *There* is the necessity of the classic of the resurrection.

THIRTEEN

Creation, Resurrection and Pastoral Care

Working ministers who have reflected on their daily experience as we have considered this double classic will have noticed that the discussion has moved between two extremes in the connection which is made between Christian faith and common human experience. On the one hand, the common experience is one of all-pervasive dependence—mature or immature, individual or corporate. The Christian faith, on the other hand, is specific in its affirmation of Jesus' resurrection. Although this belief includes ideas which can be found in religion in general, Christianity gives them distinctive definition in the classic of the resurrection.

People frequently express their feelings in generalized forms of religious behaviour. They turn up, for instance, for rites— baptisms, weddings and funerals. But the minister is often asked for quasi-magical blessings. Pastors offer themselves and the Church as focal points where the specifically Christian gospel of Christ may be found, explored and, they hope, believed. Yet in a way that seems beyond their control they also indiscriminately figure in people's half-formed world of belief. The label 'Christian' covers a range of behaviour. Much is socially acceptable—being a good neighbour and behaving well. Allied to this is a general belief in some sort of God, who benevolently oversees the universe. Jesus Christ is worth respect, although definite claims about him are left to those who are publicly religious.

But ministers who believe that they should work with those who are not already integrated into the Church soon discover that they cannot draw a simple distinction between 'false' and 'true' belief [Greinacher & Mette 1986]. Folk religion employs Christian forms and language. If ministers, therefore, appear indifferent or even hostile, they may confusingly suggest that they are rejecting the belief that they themselves profess, or, at least, that they regard it as inadequate. This is probably why Christians spend time redefining, usually to little avail, other people's use of 'their' language.

But we may go further. If Christians are honest about their faith, they cannot dispose of folk religion. On closer inspection they find its characteristics inside themselves as well as others. The notion of folk religion can become simply a projection of the parts of Christian belief and practice which believers find unmanageable. They disown them, project them into vulnerable others and deal with them there. But this is exactly the stance which the gospel condemns.

We have noted that dependence is focused at the claim which is most distinctively Christian—the resurrection. So the more Christians fail to come to terms with the dependent longing for magic, the more it will return through this classic to haunt them in their profoundest beliefs. At the heart of professed Christian faith reside aspects of the marginal types of religious behaviour which constitute the pastor's usual working material. This may explain why folk religion is such a test for the pastor and why Christians become so disturbed when the resurrection seems to be questioned. The minister is not only being confused about who he is and how he is being used (the religious figure). He is also given a sense that as he deals with these 'peripheral' matters (as they seem) he may be undermining the core classic of his faith—the resurrection.

Pastoring, Ritual and Playfulness

One thing for which people legitimately look to the Church is ritual. A church that does not worship is a contradiction in terms, and one that does not handle people's feelings and expectations through ritual is no longer distinctively a church. This is as true of requests for formal liturgical acts as it is of the approach of an individual to a minister for help. Someone asking a priest or minister for counsel does not necessarily consciously come to a religious figure. They are likely to be confused, otherwise they would not be there in the first place.

Yet the pastor is wise to ask himself why a minister of religion has been approached. Counselling services, usually confidential and often anonymous and free, are widely available. It may, of course, be that he is the last resort. But he should at least be sufficiently alert to what he may signify to be able to recognize that when many people come to a pastor, they do so in the unconscious expectation of some kind of religious response. Jesus' saying that a loving father, when someone asks for a fish, does not give him a snake, provides the paradigm for this activity (Luke 11.11). When pastors are, in however faint a fashion, implicitly invited to confirm guilt or sin and offer forgiveness or absolution, they fail if they provide only counsel or sympathy. There is a difference worth preserving between the penitent and the client, not least since this distinction often lurks in those who deliberately turn to the pastor.

Ritual plays an important part when forgiveness and absolution are sought. It is more generally important than today's somewhat limited stress on a liturgy derived from within the confines of early Christian history sometimes suggests. Like the resurrection, ritual displays the playfulness of God and its connections with the absurd and his humour. We take up special roles in order to help people make a transition from one state to another: guilty to forgiven, single to married, accompanied to bereaved, and so on. Sometimes such roles are emphasized by dress, language or style. Ministers in most traditions put on distinctive dress for ritual. For instance, a priest may put on a stole to hear a confession and pronounce absolution. The stole does not make any difference to the procedure, but it helps to establish basic conditions, such as presumed confidentiality and a formal acknowledgement that God stands behind all that is happening.

This is playful, in the sense that the dressing-up is not itself purposeful. It is one means of establishing the conditions in which work may be done. Those who on grounds of theological principle reject this may be missing a critical point in their dealings with people. Such playfulness does not trivialize. It has a very serious side, which emerges in two long-standing pictures of the pastor, as fool and as wise man, both of whom, incidentally, are usually identified by their appearance—the fool's cap and the wise person's wizened visage or beard.

The fool is given licence to say what cannot be said. He occupies a privileged position—one in which ministers regularly find themselves. Discounted as other-worldly, or somehow preserved in people's belief as immune from sullying reality, they can become the fools of this world. Their fundamental foolishness is to believe at all. But they are also envied their foolery, since it gives them permission to handle parts of life which people know are there but which they find difficult to address. When the minister knows this he can say the unspeakable without being sententious. In the full sense of the word, he 'plays' with people in a constructive play like that of God in the resurrection.

The second aspect of this playfulness is wisdom. The long tradition of wisdom begins from a firm, but critical, belief in the intrinsic value of human life and its trivia. Like the pastor with the resurrection, it switches between the peripheral life of mankind and the heart of God himself. Absurd and humorous images often make vital points about individual and social life. Jesus places himself in this line as a wise teacher when he uses parables. It is the tradition of the ridiculous story but serious issue, and of the almost cynical, worldly wise minister, who with caustic love holds a perspective for others. Lightness of touch is matched to the seriousness of the topic.

In both instances—foolishness and wisdom—playfulness is a model for pastoral practice which expresses confidence in life's trivia. The motif of resurrection undergirds the pastor's ministry in this area. He can offer interpretation to people in their confusions, hopes and fears and their longing for some sort of magic. But he does not have to deny or abandon his own religious motivation and perspective to do this. He invites people to join him in a playfulness with their lives, recognizing how responsible they are in themselves and their various roles, their relationships, relatednesses and interrelations—but not ignoring their dependent selves, to whom God has responded in this central revelation of himself.

Ritual behaviour—not just performing some ritual act, but thinking of ritual as a basis of ministry—reminds the pastor that he is a minister of God's playfulness, the gospel of resurrection. The counsellor seeks as a fellow human being to help distressed and disturbed people and works from this perspective to create new ways of coping and living. That is a rough, but sufficient, description. The pastor, however, offers — and is used to provide — something different. He, too, is a fellow human being, but in addition he is also a representative of God and of a religious view of life. There will be a gap between the belief that motivates him and what he is expected to represent, but there is always this aspect to the encounter, as well as the interrelation of two individuals and their interaction. The counsellor tries to assist people restructure their lives by gaining a new perspective on themselves and their connections with others; this is the therapeutic process. The pastor works with the same material, people and their feelings, but with a view to educating the person to see life not just with a new perspective but in the specific context of God.

That is why in the New Testament pastoring is linked with teaching: the content of the Christian faith illuminates the practice of the pastor and is included in his resource for others, even those who do not believe. But for believers and others alike the educating work of pastoral practice releases energy which can bring about major change. In Christian language this means conversion in some sense. This may be fully to Christ and the Christian Church. But at its least it can be in the way that they view themselves, others and the world in the setting of the larger context that the idea of God represents.

When the minister grasps this, two points follow. First, he need not be over-concerned about the apparent foolishness of the Christian gospel on which he bases his ministry. This is not only the foundation of his life and work; it is also what enables him to be involved with people at all. The playfulness of ritual is not just amusing; it is a latching-on point for ministry, since it is a way of affirming to ministers and those whom they meet that the context is God. The criterion by which to test any foolishness is whether it has become an end in itself. The fool may become the clown and then shift to being the idiot. That foolishness is not an asset but a liability. The test of the foolishness of God is whether it engages people's profoundest feelings, conscious and unconscious, whatever the outcome. The foolishness which is divine and which God expresses, at least in significant part, through his ministers is not a consciously self-generated stance, but derives from interaction with people's expectations. This, as we have seen, is exactly the character of the resurrection. It stands as a permanent challenge to the pastor of the creative foolishness of God as a practical notion.

The second consequence is that the minister can recover confidence in making explicit use of the gospel. His interpretation of life needs to have Christian content, not by loading on to people stories or demands, which may seem unbelievable, but by embodying the faith that these have inspired. The resurrection imbues this stance, too. It can be called a Christian classic only when it is being used. Thought of primarily in terms of function, it reminds ministers that presence and empathy alone, crucial as they are, do not satisfy people's expectations of the Church and its ministers — the hope of God. The freedom of wonder and imagination, and the large vision that can ensue, are endorsed by God in the resurrection. This constitutes the pastor's stance and the penitent's destiny.

Case Study

This instance is drawn from everyday pastoral ministry and illustrates the significance of simple ritual activity, when performed with sensitivity and with some awareness of its significance.

A woman in the parish, who had nothing directly to do with his church, asked the vicar to call because her mother was dying. Some years previously her son had been in trouble and in prison on remand. At that time the vicar had heard and visited, spending a short time with her. This, however, was the extent of formal contact. They had occasionally met in the pub, but for three years prior to this episode he had not seen her at all and had assumed that she had left the district. She lived with her mother, the other sisters being some distance away. Her phone call to the vicar included the following passage: 'Please come, vicar. Mother is dying. The doctor has been and is looking after her, but she is not settled (*sic*). Please come and settle her.'

The minister visited, was welcomed by the woman and then went in to see the dying mother. She was sedated and comfortable; there was no apparent distress. After a brief talk, the pastor performed three ritual acts: he held the dying woman's hand; he spoke reassuringly to her; and he blessed her in the name of God. The daughter thanked him and he left, promising to call in the evening. But he was prevented by another demand and that night the old lady died. Yet, although the vicar had failed to appear, there was no anger or animosity when finally he visited again. The one thing the daughter wanted him to know was that, after his visit, her mother had been much more 'settled' (*sic*). She told her sisters how splendid 'John' (*sic*) had been over the old lady's death; how helpful he 'always' (*sic*) was; and specifically how he had helped her personally.

The facts were that, although she presumed intimacy with the minister by using his first name, she had never been near the church, and her sole serious contact with him had been for about one and a half hours some four years prior to her mother's death.

The minister might have thought that proper ministry required him to try and address the woman's fantasies about him and the church, for example, by asking why she had called for him, what she really expected of him, how she saw her standing with God, or any similar questions. But whatever she, and more especially the dying woman, may have needed would probably have been overlooked. The mother had been professionally and expertly treated by her doctor, but she still wanted something that she could describe only as 'being settled'. Such settling, however, was not expected through minimal religion or generalized comforting words of religious bromide, provision of which induces guilt in ministers. The settlement seems to have been needed in the relationship between the woman and her daughter. But at the first contact this could not be exposed: the daughter was distressed as she faced certain bereavement, and the mother was dying.

The simple rituals, however, seemed to be effective for these people. The minister held the dying woman's hand and gave a blessing. Both acts had the same character; they affirmed in theological terms mother and daughter and their relationship with each other in a larger context. This was not necessarily a coherent sense of God, but more likely the vast abyss which confronts human life at the ultimate boundary of death. The women felt after this, but at that moment neither they nor, most importantly, the minister could articulate this search. We note again, therefore, the requirement that the minister, even when dealing with someone who is not a member of the Church and who has no clear intention of joining, has himself to be distinctively religious and specifically Christian. The question for pastors, therefore, when engaged in such ritual activity, is how their motivation for being there and their interpretation of what they are doing are informed by the faith that they profess.

We may now begin to perceive why ritual has pastoral effectiveness in its own right. It does not have to be complicated or ritualistic and appear quasi-magical. It does, however, have to be sufficiently congruous with the minister's profession and the expectations of those asking for such pastoring that it can be used by both. Although the minister may seem to be defended from scrutiny as he performs publicly observable ritual acts, the God whom he represents is held up for examination. This suggests, therefore, that just as ministers might need to take greater care in creating and performing the ritual of worship (on which see below), so too they may need to reflect on the way that their ritual functioning, which may at times seem to them perfunctory, has a profound effect on the lives of people. That is an issue in its own right. It is also a matter of how the Church, the gospel, and therefore ultimately God, too, have a chance of being perceived.

Pastoring Through Worship

Pastoral care based on the resurrection involves worship. This is more than inviting people to take part in services in church. In pastoral work we enable them to bring whatever aspects of their individual and corporate lives they wish [Wilkinson 1983]. We can then attempt an educational process which is programmed through a liturgical act. Baptisms, weddings and funerals are instances of how people may still expect the Church to do this. Special services for groups and communities are similarly pastoral in intent and educational in form [Carr 1985b]. They also show that, if it takes such ministry seriously, the Church can respond effectively and, contrary to what many people today suggest, with integrity.

This ministry feels uncomfortable, because the minister may be made to feel that he is colluding with people's most primitive expectations of him, of themselves and of God. These have a numbing quality, which feels threatening, inducing doubt and anxiety in the minister about the rightness of his role and even about the truth of his gospel. But when we are giving ritual shape to human experiences, the educational function does not have to be diminished for the process to be effective.

The story of Thomas from John's narrative of the resurrection is illuminating (John 20.24 — 9). Thomas represents the person with an analytic and experimental approach to belief. He is concerned with evidence and the grounds on which he is being asked to change his mind, or be converted. He also represents those who do not wish to believe. His life would be easier without the resurrection; at least he could live with and through his sense of bereavement without undue disturbance. But faced with an unpalatable interpretation which addresses itself exactly to his personal proclivities — 'Reach out and touch' — he responds without further reflection in instant adoration, the first stage of worship. The same process is followed in pastoral ministry: we engage with people on their terms, even when there is no evident wish on their part to believe what we do; deal with the issue sensitively and educationally; and through this interpretation we move to ritual expression, which will probably be unsophisticated.

The Pastor's Anxiety

Pastoral care based on creation and resurrection, therefore, draws attention first to the minister and what he feels to be expected of him rather than to the client or penitent. It emphasizes the pastor's public roles as God-person, representative of the Church and even, especially in people's unconscious minds, purveyor of some sort of magic. It also stresses the importance of our engagement with folk religion as a genuine religious expression. We may not feel comfortable with it; indeed, we probably should not. But the resurrection will not allow the pastor to dismiss it as none of the Church's concern. Thirdly, it directs us to the practical use of ritual and worship, in which there is no need to worry that the Christian faith seems to be betrayed.

But the fact is that we do worry. Many ministers are perturbed by these dimensions to their ministry, not least amid the many transitions that societies and the Churches are today undergoing. The question is how to survive as we are caught up in this welter of deeply felt, dimly grasped, but profound experiences and associated superstitions. A seminarian recently remarked that it was all very well knowing about the person of Christ and the revealed Father, but this did not help much when confronted by devotion to the bleeding heart of Jesus. The core classic of the resurrection ensures, however, that the chief betrayal in such circumstances would lie less in countenancing the debased beliefs of people than in the minister's operating without sufficient regard to his own profession of Christian faith. As we have explored in each of the pastoral sections of this study, the approach to Christian ministry is through being able to use ourselves both as what we are and what we represent for others. The clue each time is the use made of us.

If pastors are to be willing to be used, they need the model of integration in person and role that we have seen in the classics of the incarnation and the cross of Christ. But they also need more — some means of holding together the complex interactions between the minister's person and role, his life and that of others, the Church and its environment, and ultimately God and the world. In other words, they need a way of dealing with the necessary undergirding of pervasive dependence without allowing it to become stultifying. The classic of the creation and resurrection sustains this side of the minister's and the Church's life. It is the core Christian classic, which, if explored in the light of experience and ministry, reinforces the minister in his pastoral dealings with others and in his basic calling and motivation as a Christian.

FOURTEEN

Creation, Resurrection and the Disciples' Worship

The twin themes of creation and new creation are not private concerns of the Church. They intersect with common human experience and general religious belief at the point of worship. This activity is not the prerogative of the committed believer, but is shared by many, if not most, people. If prayer, as we earlier saw, is a more widespread phenomenon than we usually realize, people demonstrate a worship-like stance towards an object or person more frequently than they readily admit.

Worship as Play

A worshipper bows before God, sings his praises, rehearses his mighty acts, seeks forgiveness and renewed strength through contact with God. The whole activity is typically play, having little discernible motive and no obvious purpose. Indeed, within the Christian tradition it has usually been reprehensible to take part in worship hoping for some reward. It is the way we accept God's invitation to share his play. Movement in worship reminds us of this. Although liturgical movements have on the whole become ritualized, they still take place. For example, people may sit, stand or kneel; the minister may walk between stall, lectern, pulpit and altar. Offertory processions are central in most Eucharists. These are the residue of the primary movement that underlies worship—the dance of all creation around God.

In Christian worship we play with God in his creation. This sounds childish. It is not; but it should be childlike. We should distinguish this notion from the idea that worship is the play of God's creatures before their Creator. That view

212

emerges whenever worshippers are infantilized and encouraged to behave as children. This is childishness, which confirms immature dependence in such a way as to prevent development. God becomes a powerful, albeit benevolent, paternal figure as we abdicate to him what are properly our responsibilities and revert to childishness.

Playing with God is different. It allows us to give the widest range to our dreams and hopes. We receive permission as adults, struggling with the important and unimportant demands of life, to regress to an immature posture without feeling that this is untoward or, what is more important, that by so doing we deny our autonomy. In other words, looked at as a form of behaviour, worship enables participants to move through a structured regression to a dependent acknowledgement of God.[1] Between work and rest we can face our illusions and relate them to a deliberate, conscious sense of the realities of ourselves and our life in the created order.

Worship as Managed Regression

These remarks on Christian worship are largely familiar. But when we recognize the theological significance of dependence, worship can be revalued in the light of the process of regression.

'Regression' and 'dependence', as we have found throughout this study, together sound disturbing. 'Regression' seems pejorative; 'dependence' does not seem appropriate to adult behaviour. When brought into a discussion of the emotional experience of worship they seem unduly cold. In addition, in a society which idolizes achievement, sophistication and individualism, any sense of surrender to dependence sounds undesirable. When, however, we deny the significance of regression, we cease to develop towards that maturity which we proclaim more easily than we live.

Life consists of perpetual movement between our past and present and between our fantasies and the realities that press on us. Structured or managed regression provides the way to acknowledge these facts—our necessary dependence; our fantasized worlds, which affect our decisions and behaviour; and the curiosity which makes us human. We deliberately return to and build upon the genuine foundation of the basic psychological condition with which we are created.

Folk religion, for example, persists because in some form it is necessary for human life. Its demise has often been predicted, but it does not disappear; this is because the primitive expressions and expectations which make up that *mélange* of belief and practice are part of the underlying nature of us all. Although such religion emphasizes assurance and thus tends to encourage a stuck dependence, in practice it always includes, in however small a way, some expectation of change. Superstitious people, for example, are not solely dealing with felt anxiety. The effort to avert danger changes the way that they relate to their environment. It is, therefore, false to contrast folk religion with 'true' religion, as if the one was seeking dependable reassurance while the other stood for exploration by independent spirits seeking change. The difference between the two concerns the nature of the change expected and the way in which dependence is acknowledged and interpreted.

Regression to dependence is not, therefore, a reversion to an infantile mentality but a movement back to aspects of our origins which continue to be vital in our adult lives. It needs to be given recognition, since it provides a major way of grasping firmly the responsibility which belongs to all of us as human beings. Worship, whatever form it takes, gives distinctive form and structure to this function of necessary regression.

For example, as a congregation assembles, a number of individuals in various states of disarray, both in themselves and in their roles, come together. One may be, for instance, a mother. She has spent the week in the turmoil of home, family and many other settings. Her life has impinged upon and been affected by many others, individuals and organizations alike. She not surprisingly feels in disarray. But that experience, however personally intense, is not hers alone; we may also view her as representing other mothers in that area and the pressures upon all in that role. By allowing her to regress in a structured fashion to a dependent state, worship may gradually release this mother from the pressures of her life, both as herself and in her roles (which coincide with the confusions of others like her, whom she unwittingly represents). She is responsible for much. But she is now freed for a while to give free rein to the childlike view of the world of fantasies and illusions which lies within her.

The focus for this dependence is ultimately God, although we should not underestimate its proximate foci—the liturgy itself, the setting, or the minister. In this regressed state, however, worshippers are offered ways of reorientating themselves towards their responsibilities in God's world. Acts of worship are not merely emotional experiences. They include specific interpretation through reading, preaching and actions. Through these, people are invited to make their personal responses, which become stages towards competent living in their many roles. The mother may reorder her life as an individual person, in role or as representative of others, as she reflects upon whatever parts of her experience are uppermost and hears the interpretations and responds to them. Finally the obvious fact: services finish. The fact of ending presses the point that regression is not a state in which adults, individuals or groups, are to become fixed.

Worship, when seen in such a light—and this is not a total explanation, but it is one neglected facet of the Church's activity—addresses crucial and problematic issues of myself and my roles. It cannot be performed without deep and critical study. Indeed it may be that ministers today need to give more attention to this aspect of their role. It is becoming a commonplace that Sunday's activity is not as significant as work from Monday to Saturday, during which pastors are most likely to deal with people individually. But any such distinction proves false. We need to think carefully about the overall process of worship. It needs more thought than merely the casual adoption of whatever order is customarily used. Movement and music alike have to be co-ordinated within that process. Interpretative skills lie not just with whatever the preacher may wish to say, but in the coherence that is evidenced in all the interpretative material, readings and sermon alike.

When we see worship in this way we cannot promote it, or, as some might wish, dismiss it, as merely an other-worldly pursuit. It takes place at one of the cores of human life, where individual and society, personal disposition and public role, together with issues of autonomy, authority and responsible behaviour, all coincide and can therefore be examined and new interpretations be regularly absorbed in changed lives.

The Theological Context of Worship

We may now put this practical description of worship centrally in the theological context of the classic of the creation and resurrection. At the play of worship our dependence, which derives from our creation, is harnessed to the new creation. For, as we saw, it enables us to link our rational aspects with the irrational, and to co-ordinate our purposeful striving for achievement with the dimension of our existence which is being for its own sake—play. In more familiar Christian terms, through worship our lives are redeemed as we bring into focus the way of the cross as both God's way and ours. We are also restored as, through the proclamation of the resurrection, the consummation (when God will be all in all) is momentarily glimpsed.

Northrop Frye has expressed this in another context[2] thus: 'Now the work ethic has settled into better focus we can perhaps understand a bit more clearly than we could a century ago why *Othello* and *Macbeth* are called plays. Play is that for the sake of which work is done, the climactic sabbath vision of mankind.'

The inner connections between work and play, spirituality, prayer and worship are thus exposed. The way to outline this now is in terms both of the dynamics of human behaviour which we have been examining and of the particular approach to these that we have been using throughout this book.

Of these dependence is the most persistent—the normal or basic stance. Only if this is competently handled, therefore, can the other modes of behaviour be turned to useful ends. For example, in order to be able to fight and so achieve something people need to feel confident that the side of them that seeks basic security—that is, dependence—is being safeguarded. If not, then they are likely to revert to this and so not be able to mobilize their fight/flight dynamic to achieve success or victory. This is a familiar phenomenon when war looms. Individuals and groups turn to the Churches to guarantee a security which they know has to be discounted if they are to give their energies to fighting. As the 'fight aspects' of people and a society are geared up for war, along with the matching panic which seeks flight, people's dependence has to be reassuringly sustained and handled.

In any organization or society, different groups have to adopt roles on behalf of one another so that work can be furthered. Since all of us cannot do everything—and since we certainly cannot live at a heightened dynamic level across the spectrum—consciously, but more often unconsciously, we parcel out different functions to different groups or people. This insight, derived from Freud, was outlined by Bion. In his exploration of groups and what seems to occur between them, he speculated that there was a connection between the basic assumptions which undergird group behaviour, and social institutions. The Church, for example, embodied the dependent assumption; the Army reflected fight/flight; and the aristocracy, with its special concern about family, breeding and marriage, stood for pairing [Bion 1961]. Bion's argument was more refined than this crude presentation might imply. Today, too, these suggestions would have to be considerably modified [Khaleelee & Miller 1985], but the essential point remains: no one group or individual operates with all these dynamics at the same time. Because we are as we are as human beings, organizations become necessary and delegation (so that we can act on behalf of each other) becomes crucial.

The fragile dynamics of pairing and fight/flight are needed for achievement. They are risky and often involve pain, but we can only mobilize them when our underlying dependence is safeguarded. We have fastened these two dynamics to two Christian classics: pairing is linked to the incarnation and its outcome in the Kingdom of God; fight/flight, that double dynamic, puts Christ on the cross and endorses that way of acting and achievement as God's. Resurrection, as new creation, affirming that God is willing to acknowledge his creatures in their basic stance towards him of dependence, cannot, therefore, be a consequence of the incarnation and the cross. It stands at the core of the Christian profession, but most closely in relation to the creation. There God handles the underlying dynamic of his creation, which makes the others usable in distinctive ways for our salvation.

Christians have a persistent penchant to diminish the

significance of this. We sometimes make the resurrection a logical outcome of the incarnation — because Christ is the Son of God he must demonstrate this by a mighty act of power. At other times, too, we treat it as the vindication of the crucifixion — the way of the cross must be proved to be truly God's way before we can invite anyone to walk in it. But both these attitudes, or assumptions, have the effect of diminishing the intrinsic importance of these two classics and the intimate links which they have with common human experience. Then theological insight, as it seems, undermines pastoral ministry rather than illuminates it. Consequently pastoring is devalued and surrenders its direction and theological ground to psychotherapy or religious fundamentalism, and prayer and spirituality also lose touch with their theological roots and pastoral purpose and bewilderingly decline in significance for believers.

Notes

1   The term 'regression' describes a reversion to earlier structures of behaviour. It does not necessarily carry pejorative overtones [Freud 1900]. Reed [1978] defends its retention to describe the process involved in worship: 'The word unfortunately has overtones of pathology and infantile behaviour . . . We have retained it . . . because we suspect that the antipathy it arouses is in part a reaction to the process signified, and not just to its misleading associations' [Reed 1978, 22].

2   This quotation was given to me some years ago by the Rev. Paul Gibson, but unfortunately I have mislaid the reference.

Conclusion

———

Hence in a season of calm weather
Though inland far we be,
Our souls have sight of that immortal sea
Which brought us hither,
Can in a moment travel thither,
And see the Children sport upon the shore,
And hear the mighty waters rolling evermore.

(Wordsworth, *Intimations of Immortality*)

FIFTEEN

Still Hearing the Mighty Waters

'On the seashore of endless worlds', religion in its finer moments encourages men and women to become the 'children [who] sport upon the shore'. I have tried to help those whose task this is to see both why it is so complicated and demanding and yet why it is so vital. We have linked together the basic structures of our human life with divine revelation as this is interpreted in three great Christian classics. And we have not ignored the specific connection that the distinctive practice of discipleship makes between these two. Schematized the issues are these:

DYNAMIC	CLASSIC	PASTORAL MINISTRY	DISCIPLESHIP
Pairing	Incarnation	Using differences	Prayer
Fight/flight	Atonement	Handling projection	Spirituality
Dependence	Creation/ Resurrection	Ritual	Worship

This scheme may help locate the structure of the whole argument more easily, but it is an over-simplified way of expressing complex relations.

There is probably nothing more important confronting the Christian Churches at the present than the issue of making connections between belief and practice, between theology and the social and behavioural sciences, and between pastoring people and building up disciples. It is not merely a question of how the gospel is to be reinterpreted in our age for our contemporaries and communicated to them. T. G. A.

Baker, then Dean of Worcester, captured many people's attention in a speech to the General Synod in 1983, in which he said:

> The implication [of the ease with which the word 'God' is used] might seem to be that Christians have no difficulty today about the reality of God in the world as we have it today; that the world does not believe in that reality, but the Church does, and all that is necessary is to find the right words, the proper conviction and the correct apologetic ... Things are not quite as simple as that, and the problem concerns belief in God within the Church and not only outside it. The fact is that some, I do not say many and certainly not most, but some convinced Christians do not find it at all easy either to grasp or to communicate the reality of God in today's society. [Baker 1983, 963]

Ministers, however, on whom for good or ill the Churches rely, must take this question into account in all that they do. The problem of living is not one of finding a suitable language. Even if we were to find a perfect means of verbally communicating experience, the issue that Baker draws to our attention would remain: for everyone, whatever their religious persuasion and depth of belief, the old lines of demarcation which orientated all of us in the world are apparently dissolving, and no obvious new ones are yet emerging in their place.

By taking human behaviour and its interpretation as a key, we have found that there can be no restriction of the Christian gospel to its believers or to a sacred area alone. The problems of meaning are in Christians and others alike; the differences about being human run through all people, regardless of their particular beliefs. So, too, therefore, we may assume the work of God also pervades everything and everyone. We have noted how, in particular, the existence of persisting folk religion indicates not just facets of ordinary human life to which the Church must pay attention but also one way by which God sends messages to his Church.

By taking key Christian doctrines—the three classics—I have tried to show that the medium by which God calls his Church into existence and sustains it is also the medium by which he engages with all his human creation at a level more profound than many of us had realized. The classics therefore preserve the Church, but are also preserved by the Church for the benefit of the world. This benefit cannot be idealized: it has to be through use that they are of value to this world. And 'use' in this context means 'ministry'.

The pastoral opportunities which remain to the Churches and their ministers are not yet to be surrendered. Undoubtedly they have changed and are changing. But we abandon them too easily because they have become increasingly uncomfortable rather than see that much of the difficulty is endemic in the times in which God calls us to be faithful. If I am right that there is an intimate link between what goes on inside the individual and what is happening outside him, and between what happens inside an institution and what is occurring in its environment, and, more specifically, between churches and their human settings, then to be faithful today's Christians have no choice but to sustain *every* opportunity for encounter, whatever the cost [Hastings 1986, 660–71].

Such faithfulness is for believers its own reward. But there are also advantages in terms of liveliness of church life and stimulus of doctrinal understanding to be derived from this approach:

> The protection against . . . doctrine becoming ossified or defensively conservative lies in the extent to which the church adheres to its distinctive task. For if it does this, it will find itself permanently caught up in practical tussles which heighten the critical question of why a particular point of belief matters. [Carr 1983, 152]

The task referred to is essentially a dynamic one: the issue always facing the Churches, and their pastors in particular, is how, in the light of our own make-up and the confused feelings constantly generated in us from all sides, we can discern the prevailing dynamic in any situation, harness it for ministry, and interpret it in the light of the Christian gospel. Because that work is likely to lead to hesitation about doctrine, to soundly based experimentation about the practice of ministry, and to a stretching of personal faith and devotion to Christ, it seems to me intrinsically worthwhile.

Bibliography

Publications not originally in English are cited only in their translated version.

Freud's works are cited by title and reference to SE, *The standard edition of the complete psychological works of Sigmund Freud* (London, Routledge & Kegan Paul, 1953–1973).

Badcock, C. R. (1980), *The Psychoanalysis of Culture*. Oxford, Basil Blackwell.

Baelz, P. R. (1975), *The Forgotten Dream*. Oxford and London, Mowbrays.

Baelz, P. R. (1985), *An Integrating Theology*. London, Church Information Office.

Baker, T. G. A. (1983), Speech to the General Synod of the Church of England, in *Report of the Proceedings of the General Synod* 13.3. London, Church Information Office.

Baker, T. G. A. (1986), 'Nineham as Churchman', *Theology* 89, 339ff.

Bateson, G. (1972), *Steps to an Ecology of Mind*. London, Intertext.

Becker, E. (1964), *The Revolution in Psychiatry*. New York, Free Press.

Bettelheim, B. (1986), *The Informed Heart*. Harmondsworth, Penguin Books.

Bion, W. R. (1961), *Experiences in Groups*. London, Tavistock Publications.

Blakeslee, T. R. (1980), *The Right Brain: A New Understanding of the Unconscious Mind and the Creative Powers*. London, Macmillan.

Bowker, J. W. (1973), *The Sense of God*. Oxford, OUP.

Bowker, J. W. (1978), *The Religious Imagination and the Sense of God*. Oxford, OUP.

225

Brewster, D. (1855), *Memoirs of the Life, Writings and Discoveries of Sir Isaac Newton*. Edinburgh, T. Constable.

Brown, D. (1985), 'Bion and Foulkes: Basic assumptions and Beyond', in Pines (1985), 192ff.

Buber, M. (1937), *I and Thou*. Edinburgh, T. & T. Clark.

Busch, E. (1976), *Karl Barth*. London, SCM Press.

Campbell, A. V. (1981), *Rediscovering Pastoral Care*. London, Darton, Longman & Todd.

Carr, A. W. (1974), 'Contemporary Non-Theistic Spirituality'. *Theology* 77, 412ff.

Carr, A. W. (1983), 'A Teaching Church with a Collective Mind'. *Crucible*, Oct—Dec 1983, 148ff.

Carr, A. W. (1985a), *The Priestlike Task*. London, SPCK.

Carr, A. W. (1985b), *Brief Encounters. Pastoral Ministry Through the Occasional Offices*. London, SPCK.

Crenshaw, J. L. (1982), *Old Testament Wisdom*. London, SCM Press.

Davies, P. (1984), *Superforce: The Search for a Grand Unified Theory of Nature*. London, Unwin Paperbacks.

Davis, M., and Wallbridge, D. (1981), *Boundary and Space*. London, Karnac Books.

Deri, S. (1978), 'Transitional Phenomena: Vicissitudes of Symbolization and Creativity', in Grolnick, S. A. and Barkin, L., eds., *Between Reality and Fantasy* (New York, Aronson), 45ff.

Farrell, B. A. (1981), *The Standing of Psychoanalysis*. Oxford, OUP.

Ferenczi, S. (1916; English tr. 1952), *First Contributions to Psycho-Analysis*. London, Hogarth Press.

Fines, R. (1981), *The Psychoanalytic Vision*. New York, Free Press.

Fourez, G. (1983), *Sacraments and Passages: Celebrating the Tensions of Modern Life*. Notre Dame, Indiana, Ave Maria Press.

Freud, S. (1900), *The Interpretation of Dreams*, *SE* 4—5.

Freud, S. (1912), 'The Dynamics of Transference', *SE* 12.

Freud, S. (1913), 'The Disposition to Obsessional Neurosis', *SE* 12.

Freud, S. (1915), 'The Unconscious', *SE* 14.

Freud, S. (1925), 'An Autobiographical Study', *SE* 20.

Freud, S. (1927), *The Future of an Illusion*, *SE* 21.

Freud, S. (1930), *Civilisation and Its Discontents, SE* 21.

van Gennep, A. (1960), *The Rites of Passage*. London, Routledge & Kegan Paul.

Gill, R. (1975), *The Social Context of Theology*. London, Mowbrays.

Gill, R. (1977), *The Social Structure of Theology*. London, Mowbrays.

Gorell Barnes, G. (1984), *Working with Families*. London, Macmillan.

Greinacher, N., & Mette, N. (1986), 'Popular Religion' in *Concilium* 186. Edinburgh, T. & T. Clark.

Guntrip, H. (1971), *Psychology for Ministers and Social Workers*, 3rd edn. London, Allen & Unwin.

Hastings, A. (1986), *A History of English Christianity 1920— 1985*. London, Collins.

Hay, D. (1982), *Exploring Inner Space*. Harmondsworth, Penguin Books.

Katz, S. (1978), *Mysticism and Philosophical Analysis*. London, Sheldon Press.

Kaufmann, G. D. (1981), *The Theological Imagination*. Philadelphia, Westminster Press.

Kelly, J. N. D. (1972), *Early Christian Creeds*, 3rd edn. London, Longmans.

Khaleelee, O., and Miller, E. J. (1985), 'Beyond the Small Group: Society as an Intelligible Field of Study', in Pines (1985), 354ff.

Klein, M. (1963), *Our Adult World and Other Essays*. London, Heinemann.

Kris, E. (1952), *Psychoanalytic Explorations in Art*. New York, International Universities Press.

Küng, H. (1983), *Freud and the Problem of God*. New Haven, Yale University Press.

Laplanche, J., and Pontalis, J-B. (1973), *The Language of Psycho-Analysis*. London, Hogarth Press.

van Loewenich, W. (1976), *Luther's Theology of the Cross*. Belfast, Christian Journals.

Mahler, M. S., Pine, F. and Bergman, A. (1975), *The Psychological Birth of the Human Infant*. London, Hutchinson.

Meissner, W. W. (1983), 'Notes on the Potential Differentiation of Borderline Conditions'. *International Journal of Psychoanalytic Psychotherapy* 9, 3ff.

Meissner, W. W. (1984), *Psychoanalysis and Religious Experience*. New Haven and London, Yale University Press.

Meng, H., and Freud, E. L. eds., (1963), *Psychoanalysis and Faith: the letters of Sigmund Freud and Oskar Pfister*. New York, Basic Books.

Metz, J-B., (1981), *The Emergent Church*. London, SCM Press.

Millar, S. (1968), *The Psychology of Play*. Harmondsworth, Penguin Books.

Miller, E. J., and Rice, A. K. (1967), *Systems of Organisation*. London, Tavistock Publications.

Moltmann, J. (1974), *The Crucified God*. London, SCM Press.

Moltmann, J. (1977), *The Church in the Power of the Spirit*. London, SCM Press.

Moltmann, J. (1979), *The Future of Creation*. London, SCM Press.

Morris, C. (1984), *God-in-a-box. Christian Strategy in a Television Age*. London, Hodder & Stoughton.

Niebuhr, R. (1964), *The Nature and Destiny of Man*. New York, Scribner. (The work was originally published in 1941, but the reference is to the Preface of 1964.)

North, M. (1972), *The Secular Priests*. London, Allen & Unwin.

Pannenberg, W. (1968), *Jesus, God and Man*. London, SCM Press.

Pfister, O. (1928), 'Die Illusion einer Zukunft', *Imago* 14, 149ff. (not translated into English.)

Pines, M. ed. (1985), *Bion and Group Psychotherapy*. London, Routledge & Kegan Paul.

Polanyi, M. (1958), *Personal Knowledge*. London, Routledge & Kegan Paul.

Polya, G. (1945), *How to Solve it. A New Aspect of Mathematical Method*. Princeton, Yale University Press.

Reed, B. D. (1978), *The Dynamics of Religion: Process and Movement in Christian Churches*. London, Darton, Longman & Todd.

Rioch, M. J. (1975), 'The Work of Wilfred Bion on Groups', in Colman & Bexton (1975), pp. 21ff.

Rivkin, E. (1986), *What Crucified Jesus?*. London, SCM Press.

Rizzuto, A-M. (1979), *The Birth of the Living God*. Chicago, Chicago University Press.

Robinson, J. A. T. (1963), 'Why I Wrote It', in J. A. T. Robinson and D. L. Edwards, *The Honest to God Debate*. London, SCM Press.

Robinson, J. A. T. (1973), *The Human Face of God*. London, SCM Press.

Rycroft, C. (1968), *A Critical Dictionary of Psychoanalysis*. London, T. Nelson & Sons.

Rycroft, C. (1979), *The Interpretation of Dreams*. London, Hogarth Press.

Rycroft, C. (1985), *Psychoanalysis and Beyond*. London, Chatto & Windus.

Schafer, R. (1978), *Language and Insight*. New Haven, Yale University Press.

Schweizer, E. (1971), *Jesus*. London, SCM Press.

Shapiro, E. R. (1982a), 'The Holding Environment and Family Therapy with Acting Out Adolescents'. *International Journal of Psychoanalytic Psychotherapy* 9, 209ff.

Shapiro, E. R. (1982b), 'On Curiosity: Intrapsychic and Inter-personal Boundary Formation in Family Life'. *International Journal of Family Psychiatry* 3, 69ff.

Shapiro, E. R., and Carr, A. W. (1987), 'Disguised Counter-transference in Institutions', *Psychiatry* 50, 72ff.

Simon, U. (1967), *A Theology of Auschwitz*. London, Victor Gollancz.

Sutton-Smith, B., and Kelly, D. (1984), 'The Idealization of Play', in Smith, P. K. (ed.), *Play in Animals and Humans*. Oxford, Basil Blackwell, 305ff.

Sykes, S. W. (1984), *The Identity of Christianity*. London, SPCK.

Torrance, T. F. (1969), *Space, Time and Incarnation*. Oxford, OUP.

Torrance, T. F. (1976), *Space, Time and Resurrection*. Edinburgh, Handsel Press.

Tracy, D. (1981), *The Analogical Imagination*. London, SCM Press.

Vanstone, W. H. (1982), *The Stature of Waiting*. London, Darton, Longman & Todd.

Wainwright, G. (1980), *Doxology: A Systematic Theology*.

London, Epworth Press.

Wallace, E. R. (1983), *Freud and Anthropology: A History and Reappraisal.* New York, International University Press.

Wiles, M. (1976), 'The Unassumed is the Unhealed', in *Working Papers on Doctrine.* London, SCM Press, pp. 108ff.

Wiles, M. F. (1982), *Faith and the Mystery of God.* London, SCM Press.

Wilkinson, A. (1978), *The Church of England and the First World War.* London, SPCK.

Wilkinson, A. (1983), 'Are We Really the Body of Christ?'. *Theology* 86, pp. 113ff.

Wilkinson, A. (1986), *Dissent or Conform? War, Peace and the English Churches 1900—1945.* London, SCM Press.

Winnicott, D. W. (1951), 'Transitional Objects and Transitional Phenomena' in *The Maturational Process and the Facilitating Environment.* London, Hogarth Press, 1965.

Winnicott, D. W. (1971), *Playing and Reality.* London, Tavistock Publications.

Young, F. (1975), *Sacrifice and the Death of Christ.* London, SPCK.

Young, F. (1982), *Can These Dry Bones Live?* London, SCM Press.

Zinner, J., and Shapiro, R. (1972), 'Projective Identification as a Mode of Perception in Families of Adolescents', *International Journal of Psychoanalysis* 53, 523ff.

Index

231